MW00614913

GREAT WITH GOD

POCKET GUIDE

POWER THROUGH PRAYER

The Great with God Pocket Guide: Power Through Prayer. The Great with God Series. Uniquely arranged by Robert Leatherwood.

Published by Great with God Ministries, 14903 Knotty Pine Place, Tampa, FL 33625

Printed in the United States of America. First printing, December 2019. Visit www.GreatWithGod.com to purchase bulk orders.

ISBN: 978-1-7325501-5-5

(NLT) Unless otherwise indicated, all Scripture quotations are taken from the Holy Bible, New Living Translation, copyright © 1996, 2004, 2015 by Tyndale House Foundation. Used by permission of Tyndale House Publishers, Carol Stream, Illinois 60188. All rights reserved.

(KJV) The Holy Bible, King James Version.

(NKJV) New King James Version. The New King James Version is an English translation of the Bible first published in 1982 by Thomas Nelson.
(NIV) Holy Bible, New International Version. Copyright 1973, 1978, 1984, International Bible Society.

(CEV) The Contemporary English version is a translation of American Bible Society's that was first published in 1995.

(AMP) 1965 English Bible translation by Zondervan and The Lockman Foundation; a revision of the 1901 American Standard Version.

Interior design and typesetting/formatting by Jodi Giddings; cover art by Sammie Wheaton; interior art by Gwendy Gayle Delos Santos.

Editing consulting team: Brad and Linda Miller, Sue Forster.

The source for the titles of most of the Commands of Christ are borrowed from the Commands of Christ Curriculum (IBLP).

Faith In Action assignments inspired by Operation Lightforce.

Various Index Prayer Wheels inspired by many sources; see references.

Composed for the Glory of God
that the world may know
the authentic nature of
the One True Living God
and that His disciples might learn
to enjoy the pleasure of His company
by cultivating a dynamic prayer life

INTRODUCTION

INTRODUCTION

HOW TO READ THIS BOOK FOR ALL IT'S WORTH

Did you ever want to do something great for God? There is a prerequisite. Great works require great faith. Faith grows when it's nurtured. Consider this devotional as a guide, coaching you through the key ingredients that cause your faith to grow and thus prepare you to do Great works *for* God as you become Great *with* God. **The formula is predictable, the scriptures say, "Come close to God, and God will come close to you (JAM. 4:8)."** That's when growth happens.

HOW THE BOOK IS ORGANIZED

You cannot trust God if you do not know what he is like. Trust grows as we learn more about the nature of God.

Within these pages are 52 ways to help you know God better. Enclosed are the most prominent attributes that God has revealed to us about Himself. He wants you to know Him. And he has revealed Himself through the scriptures in His names, titles, roles, and attributes. Now these 52 key attributes have been compiled together for your convenience into this very book.

The book is organized according to the traditional under-standing of the Christian trinity: God the Father, God the Son, and God the Holy Spirit. Also included is how it is that God expresses his nature through the life of his followers. There are seven divisions under the heading **"The Image of God"** and are presented as follows:

SECTION ONE: THE IMAGE OF GOD

- ○ **God the Father**
  - **Imago Dei**—God revealed through various **attributes**; names, titles, and roles.
  - The Jehovah Names of God—God revealed through various versions of his **name.**

- ○ **God the Son**
  - Jesus Image—God revealed through Jesus **attributes**; roles and titles.
  - The Seven "I Am" Sayings of Jesus the Messiah. God revealed through Jesus' **names.**

- ○ **God the Holy Spirit**
  - The Fruit of the Spirit—God revealed through the **attributes** of the Holy Spirit.
  - The Sevenfold Spirit of God—God revealed through the **names** of the Holy Spirit.

- ○ **God in His Disciples**
  - The Beatitudes—God revealed through the **attributes** of His Disciples.

*A note about **The Image of God:** God always acts in complete harmony with his nature. It is a principle God designed into the very fabric of creation. He said, "Let the land sprout with vegetation—every sort of seed-bearing plant, and trees that grow seed-bearing fruit. These seeds will then produce the kinds of plants and trees from which they came. And that is what happened (GEN. 1:11)." Here we see a principle; that is a reflection of the very nature of God. *God Himself acts in complete harmony with his nature. Out of the essence of God He commands us.* Because God is love, He commands us to love. Because God is holy, God commands us to be holy. Etc.

SECTION TWO: THE COMMANDS OF CHRIST

Please note a Command of Christ has been paired with each of the 52 key attributes of God. Christ spoke 52 different times, in the command tense, that is after you, that account for duplicates throughout the gospels. Now you hold in your hand the 52 Commands of Christ. These are his teachings; these are his doctrines. This is also a vital component of this book because it answers one of life's most critical questions: How do you know when you've made a disciple of Christ? The answer is revealed by Christ's words Himself when he said, "Go into all the world and make disciples of all nations, baptizing them in the name of the Father, Son and Holy Spirit and **teach them to obey everything I have commanded you**" (MATT. 28:19-20).

You cannot obey what you don't know. To be a disciple of Christ is to know his commands and to strive to obey them. The first step to obeying them is to keep his commandment continuously before our eyes. Once again you now have that resource in your hands. Then we memorize them that we might meditate on them. Finally, if we are going to be mighty in spirit and great in faith, we must make application to our lives. "Faith without works is dead" (JAM. 2:17).

*A note about the pairings of the Commands of Christ with the Image of God: while *most pairings with the Image of God are obviously harmonized* (example: since God Himself is holy, we are encouraged and commanded to live holy), *sometimes the pairings are antithetical.* Example: God is Judge has been paired with the command of Christ, Judge Not.

SECTION THREE: THE PROMISES OF GOD

When you know God and obey Christ's commands, then the promises and blessings of God begin to manifest in you, through you, and to you. When you are living in alignment with God, you will be blessed in due season. You will live a blessed life; in fact, the scriptures teach that the blessings of God will actually seek you out, find you, and overtake you.

Why promises come true?
- When you're living in alignment with God, you are living in your sweet spot; regardless of the outward appearance of circumstances, all things are indeed sovereignly working together for your good. Even pain and suffering are redeemed.
- The law of sowing and reaping will eventually begin to manifest in due season (both good seed and bad seed): *"Be not deceived; God is not mocked: for whatsoever a man sows, that shall he also reap. For he that sows to his flesh shall of the flesh reap corruption; but he that sows to the Spirit shall of the Spirit reap life everlasting"* (Gal. 6:7–8).

Just wait: the Three Laws of the Harvest will eventually begin to manifest:

1. You always reap what you sow
2. You reap more than you sow
3. You reap at another season than you sowed

SECTION FOUR: MEMORIZE THE KEY VERSE
Choose a memory verse. Choose your favorite verse from the three sections of the attribute-of-the-week (Image of God, Commands of Christ, Promises.) **That becomes your key verse to memorize for the week.** Write it down on a note card. Rehearse it in your mind over and over. Your goal is to memorize this verse for this week. This is done through intentional repetition. Carry it with you everywhere you go. Repeat it throughout the week and think deeply about it.

SECTION FIVE: "LIVING IN ALIGNMENT WITH THE NATURE OF GOD"

In this section are questions for self-evaluation. They can be discussed in a small group/family gathering or individually as a point of contemplation. Many of the questions can be answered from the scriptures included, but not all. Some questions were designed to lead toward thoughtful application; others require further search from the scriptures.

SECTION SIX: FAITH IN ACTION

These creative assignments were also designed in alignment with the nature of God. They provide practical opportunities for application in your spheres of influence. Faith with works is a glory to God. Jesus said, "In the same way, let your good deeds shine out for all to see, so that everyone will praise your heavenly Father" (MATT. 5:16). There are hundreds of ideas to shine brightly for Christ. So don't hesitate to go to the website, **www.GreatWithGod.com,** to get more creative applications.

*Please note that these **Faith in Action** assignments are filled with variety:

- Carried out at different locations: home, school, work, community, or church.
- Be a blessing to others
- Written encouragement
- Gifts to be given
- Random acts of kindness
- Strategic prayer

SECTION SEVEN: THE PRAYER GUIDE: APPEAL TO HEAVEN

Praying in alignment with the name of God/essence of God. Prayer becomes exciting and faith-filled when praying in his name. Think of how God delights to answer each prayer made in His name. To pray in the name of God is to pray after the likeness of His nature. In this way, the power of God is unleashed through the faith-filled prayers of his children.

*A note about the Prayer Indexes (easily recognizable by their graphic artwork; 16 total indexes): an index is an outline for praying. And most scholars agree that the Lord's Prayer was designed as an index prayer. The index becomes your guide through your devotional prayer time. This is an integral part of this devotional experience. Our hope is to add fervency and effectiveness to your prayers by engaging your spirit, mind, heart and body in a creative variety of scripture-driven index prayers. You will learn to recognize them and enjoy them. A new prayer index accompanies each of the seven headings (The Image of God). For example: the Imago Dei (division one) is paired with the Lord's Prayer Wheel Index.

*Note the indexes paired with the various book divisions:

- Imago Dei—The Lord's Prayer Index
- Jehovah Names of God—The Tabernacle Index
- High Priestly Blessing Index
- Jesus Image—High Priestly Blessing
- The I Am Sayings of Christ—"R" You Praying Index
- Fruit of the Spirit—Various Indexes
- The Sevenfold Spirit—The Ripple Index
- The Beatitudes—Body Position Index

*Also note that while this book does offer written prayers, these are contributed so as to be catalytic in nature. The idea behind the index prayers is:

- To move the disciple of Christ beyond "rote" praying.
- To move beyond reading someone else's prayer.
- To develop a personal communion with God.

- That you might become great with God.
- That your spirit life would soar with prayers from your heart.

The Index then becomes helpful as a starting point and will help you know what to pray next. The prayer guide can be used in the following manner. Take this example from The Lord's Prayer Index:

1. Pray completely through the provided index prayer each day; i.e. the Lord's Prayer.
2. Then pray specifically the index theme as listed according to the day of the week; i.e. Sunday—Thy Name.
3. Then use "Thy Name" as a catalyst for your own Prayers. Think of the various names of God, perhaps even alphabetically. Such as: **A.** Almighty, Abba, Adoni. **B.** Bread of life, Beloved. **C.** Creator, Chief Shepherd. Etc.

Let the names guide your praying. Thank Him and praise Him for how His attributes have benefited you. Also be mindful of how this attribute is what you and others need now. Our hope is to give you a running head start so that you will be off and praying fervently and effectively. Your goal for your devotional time is 15 minutes daily, with five minutes of prayer each day, decidedly focused on the index theme. (Sure you can pray longer, but learn to crawl before you walk).

Saturday, pray through the entire prayer index in 35 minutes.

*Note about the prayer indexes: visit our online website at **www.GreatWithGod.com**. You may download the free guide on how to lead a group using an index prayer wheel for your family, small groups, and churches. Video instructions and examples also available online.

THE PHILOSOPHY BEHIND THE BOOK

The aim is to focus on transformational habits; these are the foundational visions of the use of *Great With God*. We believe that transformation comes to believers from internalizing the word of God and by being in His presence. This curriculum was composed that you might experience the joy of maintaining a living communion with your Maker. Finally, we believe that change comes through the application of practicing both prayer and action.

Habits are the tools that bring transformation. Please make a note that this is a daily devotional divided into 52 weeks. The idea behind the creation of this book is to develop a repetitive habit of being in scripture and prayer, resulting in growing faith. Here is the desired outcome of following such a routine: scripture fed, spirit led, promise-based prayer, manifesting with you becoming great with God. Your destiny is to be best friends with God, to live in oneness of spirit, to maintain a living communion with God your father. By repetitively reading, memorizing, and praying the same attribute for a week at a time, you create a healthy environment for these truths to transform you.

Repetition is the core of learning. *Great with God* was designed carefully and thoughtfully with repetition in mind.

- Repetition is how we grow strong in our bodies.
- Repetition is how we grow strong in our character.
- Repetition is how we grow mighty in spirit.
- Our soul is transformed by the repetition of the word of God renewing our minds.
- Our hearts are transformed as we repeatedly spend time in God's presence.

SO WHEN DO I/WE START? OPTIONS TO CONSIDER

Your prayer commitment is for the duration of a year regardless of the starting point.

- With a group? Get the group's (family) consent and start together.
- National Day of Prayer? Start the day of your city's event; it is your launch date.
- Start the New Year, January 1, 20xx.
- Individual? Start the day you get this book.
- Individual? Start on any Sunday.
- Write your start date here_____. You may also go to the website and formalize your engagement by registering: "Join the Committed." For those participating in the National Year of Prayer you may go to www.nationalyearofprayer.com and Stand in the G.A.P. Join with other (Great Appeal Partners)—disciples with a kindred spirit, committed to standing in the gap for the kingdom of God and this nation.

*A note about Wisbit Tips: These tips are added to give insight into the best practices of prayer. They are found completely randomly throughout the book. However, if you register online you can receive periodic emails—Wisbit Tips—to encourage you along this yearlong journey.

Special editions: *Great With God* is partnering with the National Day of Prayer to equip disciples for yearlong prayer. Go to **www.GreatWithGod.com** for more resources, including alternative editions for students, children, and artists.

*How to use *Great With God* as a family devotional or to facilitate small group usage also found online.

CONTENTS

TABLE OF CONTENTS

*Please note that a Command of Christ marked "CC" has been paired with each of the 52 Attributes of God.[1]

TABLE OF CONTENTS

TABLE OF CONTENTS

TABLE OF CONTENTS

THE BEATITUDES
BODY POSITION ALIGNMENT INDEX

GOD THE FATHER

THE IMAGE OF GOD

1 Covenant Maker   6 Grace
2 Father   7 Order
3 Almighty   8 Judge
4 Freedom   9 Eternal
5 Creator

PRAY USING THE LORD'S PRAYER INDEX WHEEL

YOUR GOAL: PRAY THROUGH THE LORD'S PRAYER EACH DAY, AND THEN PRAY FOR 5 MINUTES CONCERNING THE INDEX THEME ASSIGNED EACH DAY. USE THE PRAYER GUIDE AT THE END OF EACH CHAPTER TO HELP YOU GET STARTED.

ON SATURDAY, COMPLETE YOUR MEDITATION FOR THE WEEK BY PRAYING COMPLETELY THROUGH THE PRAYER WHEEL INDEX IN 35 MINUTES

WISBIT TIP: START YOUR PRAYER TIME BY ASKING THE HOLY SPIRIT TO HELP YOU PRAY.

THE LORD'S PRAYER INDEX WHEEL

Our Father, who art in heaven, hallowed be **Thy Name**. **Thy Kingdom** come. **Thy Will** be done in earth as it is in heaven. **Give Us** this day our daily bread, and **Forgive Us** our trespasses, as we forgive those who trespass against us. **Lead Us** not into temptation, but **Deliver Us** from evil: For thine is the kingdom, and the power, and the glory, forever. Amen. (Matt. 6:9-13, kjv)

Inspiration for the Lord's Prayer Index Wheel from Dick Woodward, Sermon on the Mount, Mini Bible College.[2]

1

Covenant Maker

THE IMAGE OF GOD: "For example, there was God's promise to Abraham. Since there was no one greater to swear by, God took an oath in his own name, saying: 'I will certainly bless you, and I will multiply your descendants beyond number.' Then Abraham waited patiently, and he received what God had promised. Now when people take an oath, they call on someone greater than themselves to hold them to it. And without any question that oath is binding. God also bound himself with an oath, so that those who received the promise could be perfectly sure that he would never change his mind" (HEB. 6:13-17).

▪ "For the LORD your God is a merciful God; he will not abandon you or destroy you or forget the solemn covenant he made with your ancestors" (DEUT. 4:31).

▪ "For this is my blood, which confirms the covenant between God and his people. It is poured out as a sacrifice to forgive the sins of many" (MATT. 26:28).

— FOLLOW ME —

THE COMMAND OF CHRIST: Jesus called out to them, "Come, follow me, and I will show you how to fish for people!" (MATT. 4:19).

▪ "For God called you to do good, even if it means suffering, just as Christ suffered for you. He is your example, and you must follow in his step" (1 PET. 2:21).

▪ "Follow my example, as I follow the example of Christ" (1 COR. 11:1).

▪ "Whoever does not take up their cross and follow me is not worthy of me" (MATT. 10:38).

1 GOD'S PROMISES: TO KEEP HIS COVENANT AND FORGIVE US

▪ "But if we are living in the light, as God is in the light, then we have fellowship with each other, and the blood of Jesus, his Son, cleanses us from all sin. But if we confess our sins to him, he is faithful and just to forgive us our sins and to cleanse us from all wickedness" (1 Jn. 1:7-9).

▪ "And so, dear brothers and sisters, we can boldly enter heaven's Most Holy Place because of the blood of Jesus. By his death, Jesus opened a new and life-giving way through the curtain into the Most Holy Place" (Heb. 10:19-20).

✓ ── LIVING IN ALIGNMENT WITH THE COVENANT MAKER ──

☐ What is the difference between a covenant and contract?
☐ What does God communicate by making both a promise and an oath concerning His covenant?
☐ What blessings came to Abraham through God's covenant?
☐ What blessings come to me by way of God's Covenant through Christ?
☐ What are my covenant responsibilities to God?

FAITH IN ACTION: COMMITMENT

God makes covenant promises to you. Consider making a promise to God to stay with this devotional each week for the next 52 weeks. Levels of commitment:

▪ Read and pray one attribute of God (three pages) once a day for each week.

▪ Memorize the key verse each week

▪ Fulfill the faith action assignments each week

More ideas at GreatWithGod.com

Appeal to Heaven: Use the **Lord's Prayer Index** to acknowledge the image of God as Covenant Maker.

Sunday: Your Name. I praise Your name because with Your oath çou made Yourself signer and guarantor. I honor Your name because You make promises and You keep them.

Monday: Your Kingdom. You swore to Abraham that all nations would be blessed through this covenant with him. I ask that the blessing of Your covenant would come to all nations in our lifetime.

Tuesday: Your Will. Lord, I know that it is Your will that none should perish but that all people might be saved. Let Your will be done on earth among the nations. May Your salvation come to this generation.

Wednesday: Give Us. Father, because we are in a covenant relationship, I ask You to provide the things I need to sustain me this day. Give me today the grace to believe Your covenant and grace to fulfill my responsibilities.

Thursday: Forgive Us. Lord, You said if we are faithful to confess our sins You are faithful and just to forgive us our sins. Hear now my confession of sins of thought, word, deed and motive.

Friday: Lead Us. You are the covenant maker and covenant keeper. Today I pledge my life back to You. Lead me today in paths of righteousness. I want to live for You, at Your direction. Lead me today and I will follow.

Saturday: Deliver Us. I resist the evil one in the name and through the blood of Jesus Christ, for it is written that the saints of God overcame the devil by the word of their testimony and by the blood of the Lamb. Through this covenant I belong to God.

Father

THE IMAGE OF GOD: "Do not call anyone your father; for One is your Father, He who is in heaven" (MATT. 23:9).

▪ "After this manner therefore pray ye: Our Father which art in heaven, Hallowed be thy name. Thy kingdom come. Thy will be done in earth, as it is in heaven. Give us this day our daily bread. And forgive us our debts, as we forgive our debtors. And lead us not into temptation, but deliver us from evil: For thine is the kingdom, and the power, and the glory, for ever. Amen" (MATT. 6:9-13. KJV).

▪ "Father to the fatherless, defender of widows—this is God, whose dwelling is holy"(12 Ps. 68:5).

▪ "And have you forgotten the encouraging words God spoke to you as his children? He said, 'My child, don't make light of the LORD's discipline, and don't give up when he corrects you. For the LORD disciplines those he loves, and he punishes each one he accepts as his child'" (HEB. 12:5-6).

— HONOR YOUR PARENTS —

THE COMMAND OF CHRIST: "For instance, God says, 'Honor your father and mother,' and, 'Anyone who speaks disrespectfully of father or mother must be put to death'" (MATT. 15:4).

▪ "Children, always obey your parents, for this pleases the Lord" (COL. 3:20).

▪ "Honor your father and mother, as the LORD your God commanded you. Then you will live a long, full life in the land the LORD your God is giving you" (DEUT. 5:16).

2   GOD'S PROMISES: TO CARE FOR HIS CHILDREN AS A GOOD FATHER

▪ "If you then, being evil, know how to give good gifts unto your children, how much more will your Father who is in heaven give good things to those who ask Him?" (MATT. 7:11)

▪ "For as many as are led by the Spirit of God, these are sons of God. For you did not receive the spirit of bondage again to fear, but you received the Spirit of adoption, by whom we cry out, 'Abba, Father.' The Spirit Himself bears witness with our spirit, that we are children of God, and if children, then heirs—heirs of God, and joint-heirs with Christ, if indeed we suffer with Him, that we may also be glorified together" (ROM. 8:14-17).

✓   —— LIVING IN ALIGNMENT WITH GOD OUR FATHER ——

☐ What does it mean to me to have God as my father?

☐ What can I expect to receive from God as my father?

☐ Have you ever been disciplined by God? What happened? What does that indicate?

☐ How does my spirit bear witness that I belong to God?

☐ Based on my behavior, would others come to the conclusion that God is my Father? In what way?

☐ Am I about my Father's business?

FAITH IN ACTION: HONOR YOUR FATHER

▪ Honor your dad with a gift card and a personal note. List something you're grateful to him for, then put it in the mail. A grandfather or male mentor can be substituted if necessary.

More ideas at GreatWithGod.com

Appeal to Heaven: Use the **Lord's Prayer Index** to acknowledge the image of God as Your Father.

Sunday: Your Name. Father, I thank You and I praise You that I can call You father. I trust that You have my best interests in mind in all that You allow to happen to me. I love You. Thank You for adopting me into Your family. I'm glad to know I have a dad like You.

Monday: Your Kingdom. As a father rules His house, even so come and rule my house. Come rule my life.

Tuesday: Your Will. As a father reserves the right to make the final decisions for his household, I surrender to You. I give You the right to make the final decisions in my life.

Wednesday: Give Us. My eyes look to You, for as the Scripture says, You know what I need even before I ask. Father, I trust You t

Thursday: Forgive Us. Father, take pity on me, Your child, and forgive me for my foolish, rebellious heart. Forgive me for being so slow to trust You.

Friday: Lead Us. Father, I need Your guiding eye to show me the right path. Teach me the way I should go. Enlighten me with sound judgment.

Saturday: Deliver Us. Like a good father who rescues his captured son, rescue me when I stray too far away f rom You. Keep me f rom the plots the wicked have set for me. Since You are my father, now I have a new heritage. I am Your child, so deliver me from the generational sins of my earthly forefathers.

3

Almighty

THE IMAGE OF GOD: "When Abram was ninety-nine years old, the LORD appeared to him and said, 'I am El-Shaddai – 'God Almighty.' Serve me faithfully and live a blameless life'" (GEN. 17:1).

▪ "For, at just the right time Christ will be revealed from heaven by the blessed and only Almighty God, the King of all kings and Lord of all lords. He alone can never die, and He lives in light so brilliant that no human can approach Him. No human eye has ever seen Him nor ever will. All honor and power to Him forever! Amen" (1 TIM. 6:15-16).

▪ "I am the Alpha and the Omega—the beginning and the end," says the Lord God. "I am the one who is, who always was, and who is still to come—the Almighty One" (REV. 1:8).

—— ASK IN FAITH ——

THE COMMAND OF CHRIST: Then Jesus told them, "I tell you the truth, if you have faith and don't doubt, you can do things like this and much more. You can even say to this mountain, 'May you be lifted up and thrown into the sea,' and it will happen. You can pray for anything, and if you have faith, you will receive it" (MATT. 21:21-22).

▪ "But when you ask him, be sure that your faith is in God alone. Do not waver, for a person with divided loyalty is as unsettled as a wave of the sea that is blown and tossed by the wind. Such people should not expect to receive anything from the Lord" (JAM. 1:6-7).

▪ "So then faith comes by hearing, and hearing by the word of God" (ROM.10:17 NKJV).

- "Now all glory to God, who is able, through His mighty power at work within us, to accomplish infinitely more than we might ask or think" (Eph. 3:20).
- "And you shall remember the Lord your God, for it is He who gives you power to get wealth, that He may establish His covenant which he swore to your fathers, as it is this day" (Deut. 8:18)
- "Then call on me when you are in trouble, and I will rescue you, and you will give me glory" (Ps. 50:15).
- "And this is the confidence we have in him, that if we ask for anything according to his will, he hears us" (1 Jn. 5:14 kjv).

✓   ── **LIVING IN ALIGNMENT WITH GOD ALMIGHTY** ──

☐ What does it mean that God is almighty?
☐ What is faith?
☐ What can I do to grow my faith?
☐ What obstacle keeps me from trusting God?
☐ In what ways does God answer my prayers?
☐ In times of trouble, do I ask God for help as my first plan?

FAITH IN ACTION: FAST FOR A BREAKTHROUGH

- **Fasting.** Go without food (do drink water) for 24 hours. The idea is to disconnect from the world for a day and use the spare time (formerly mealtime and recreational time) to seek God. Through fasting, try to discern which mountain He wants to move through you. Ask Almighty God to make the impossible possible.

More ideas at GreatWithGod.com

APPEAL TO HEAVEN: Use the **Lord's Prayer Index** to acknowledge the image of God as Almighty.

SUNDAY: YOUR NAME. Almighty God, this is the most awesome description of who You are. I humble myself before You. It is both an amazing and a comforting thought that the almighty God cares for me. Thank You.

MONDAY: YOUR KINGDOM. I believe You are completely sovereign. And while I rest in Your redemption, I pray even as You taught me to pray, let Your kingdom come, let Your rule be established throughout the earth.

TUESDAY: YOUR WILL. God Almighty, cause the leaders of my nation, state and city to align themselves with Your revealed holy laws.

WEDNESDAY: GIVE US. Almighty God, there is no other God like You, who lovingly provides for His people. Give me this day my portion food and grace.

THURSDAY: FORGIVE US. God, I do not deserve Your forgiveness. I throw myself at Your mercy. Forgive me according to the multitude of Your tender mercies.

FRIDAY: LEAD US. Lord God, You are almighty. Is anything too difficult for You? Open and close the right doors of opportunity for me with Your great power. There is no door shut that You cannot open. Guide me today by opening and closing doors for me.

SATURDAY: DELIVER US. You are King of kings and Lord of lords and there is no power of darkness that is greater than You. Deliver me from every demonic principality and free my soul from the sins that so easily beset me.

4 *Freedom*

THE IMAGE OF GOD: "For the Lord is the Spirit, and wherever the Spirit of the Lord is, there is freedom" (2 COR. 3:17).

▪ "So God created man in His own image; in the image of God He created him; male and female He created them. Then God blessed them, and God said to them, "Be fruitful and multiply; fill the earth and subdue it; have dominion over the fish of the sea, over the birds of the air, and over every living thing that moves on the earth" (GEN. 1:27-28).

▪ "I will walk in freedom, for I have devoted myself to your commandments" (Ps. 119:45).

▪ "… choose today whom you will serve. Would you prefer the gods your ancestors served beyond the Euphrates? …But as for me and my family, we will serve the LORD" (JOSH. 24:15).

— DO UNTO OTHERS —

THE COMMAND OF CHRIST: "Do to others whatever you would like them to do to you. This is the essence of all that is taught in the law and the prophets" (MATT. 7:12).

▪ Always be humble and gentle. Be patient with each other, making allowance for each other's faults because of your love" (EPH. 4:2).

▪ "Give, and you will receive. Your gift will return to you in full—pressed down, shaken together to make room for more, running over, and poured into your lap. The amount you give will determine the amount you get back" (LUKE 6:38).

▪ "Don't look out only for your own interests, but take an interest in others, too" (PHIL. 2:4).

- "Jesus said to the people who believed in him, "You are truly My disciples if you remain faithful to My teachings. And you will know the truth, and the truth will set you free" (JN. 8:31-32).
- "Pure and genuine religion in the sight of God the Father means caring for orphans and widows in their distress and refusing to let the world corrupt you" (JAM. 1:27).
- "The Spirit of the LORD is upon me, for he has anointed me to bring good news to the poor. He has sent me to proclaim that captives will be released…"(LUKE 4:18)

✓
—— LIVING IN ALIGNMENT WITH FREEDOM ——

- ☐ What does it mean for me to be created in the image of God, specifically concerning the attribute of freedom?
- ☐ Have I ever considered that free will is a gift from God emanating out of His very nature? What does that mean?
- ☐ What action can I take today that aligns me with God's desire for His people to be free?
- ☐ How can I live in a consistent lifestyle of moral freedom?
- ☐ How can I be free and a slave to Christ at the same time?
- ☐ Do you know of a widow or orphan that lives near you?

FAITH IN ACTION: BE A FREEDOM AGENT

defend, serve, deliver, and provide for widows and orphans, through you as His agent. Play offense: Find away to serve and provide for orphans and widows (near or far). **Near:** make a visit, offer practical service (i.e. mow a yard). **Far:** Help to build an orphanage or sponsor a child (overseas).

More ideas at GreatWithGod.com

APPEAL TO HEAVEN: Use the **Lord's Prayer Index** to acknowledge the nature of God as freedom.

SUNDAY: YOUR NAME. Heavenly Father, at the core of who You really are is freedom. Everything else about You springs forth from Your nature of freedom. So I freely give You praise for You have made me in freedom after Your very image.

MONDAY: YOUR KINGDOM. Lord, by freedom of choice I lay down all my selfish ambition and I pray that Your rule will come to every part of my life. Let Your kingdom works manifest through me.

TUESDAY: YOUR WILL. God of freedom, I pray specifically not my will but let Your will be done freely, both in and through my life.

WEDNESDAY: GIVE US. Lord, I join the with the prayers of Your people who live in poverty and are asking You for their own house of prayer. Lord grant that church buildings be funded and built in every nation.

THURSDAY: FORGIVE US. I pray that You would give the peoples of this world the gift of eternal life. Grant the gift of repentance to those who live at the ends of the earth.

FRIDAY: LEAD US. Lord, I realize You have given me freedom to choose, but today I ask You for the wisdom to choose wisely and to discern Your path for my life. Lead me today.

SATURDAY: DELIVER US. Deliver me from the power of sin, that I might live in the freedom You came to give me.

5

Creator

THE IMAGE OF GOD: "Christ is the visible image of the invisible God. He existed before anything was created and is supreme over all creation, for through Him God created everything in the heavenly realms and on earth. He made the things we can see and the things we can't see—such as thrones, kingdoms, rulers, and authorities in the unseen world. Everything was created through Him and for Him. He existed before anything else, and He holds all creation together. Christ is also the head of the church which is His body. He is the beginning, supreme over all who rise from the dead. So He is first in everything" (Col 1:15-18).

▪ "In the beginning the Word already existed. The Word was with God, and the Word was God. He existed in the beginning with God. God created everything through him, and nothing was created except through him. The Word gave life to everything that was created, and his life brought light to everyone" (JN. 1:1-4).

▪ "Let every created thing, give praise to the Lord, for He issued His command, and they came into being" (Ps. 148:5).

— WORSHIP GOD ONLY —

THE COMMAND OF CHRIST: "Next, the devil took him to the peak of a very high mountain and showed him all the kingdoms of the world and their glory. 'I will give it all to you,' he said, 'if you will kneel down and worship me.' 'Get out of here, Satan,' Jesus told him. 'For the Scriptures say, "You must worship the LORD your God and serve only him"'" (MATT. 4:8-10).

▪ "You shall have no god before me" (DEUT. 5:7).

▪ "So God created human beings in his own image. In the image of God he created them; male and female he created them. Then God blessed them and said, "Be fruitful and multiply. Fill the earth and govern it. Reign over the fish in the sea, the birds in the sky, and all the animals that scurry along the ground" (GEN. 1:27-28).

▪ "For ever since the world was created, people have seen the earth and sky. Through everything God made, they can clearly see his invisible qualities—his eternal power and divine nature. So they have no excuse for not knowing God" (ROM. 1:20).

✓   — LIVING IN ALIGNMENT WITH THE CREATOR —

☐ How convinced am I that God created everything just as He said He did?

☐ What is an idol?

☐ What is a dynamic equivalent of an idol in our society?

☐ How can I show appreciation for what God has created?

☐ When I face a need do I turn to God first? What do I turn to first?

☐ Why would someone choose to worship an idol?

FAITH IN ACTION: REMEMBRANCE STONE

▪ Worship the creator, not the creation. Write the word, *faith*, on a rock with a sharpie. Place the rock where you will see it often. Use it as a continual reminder that an invisible God created all that exists and that He alone is worthy of our worship, praise, love, and thanksgiving.

More ideas at GreatWithGod.com

APPEAL TO HEAVEN: Use the **Lord's Prayer Index** to acknowledge the image of God as creator.

SUNDAY: YOUR NAME. Let every created thing give praise to the Lord, for He issued His command, and they came into being. He holds all creation together and His name should be praised.

MONDAY: YOUR KINGDOM. Christ is supreme over all creation, for through Him God created everything in the heavenly realms and on earth. He made the things we can see and the things we can't see—such as thrones, kingdoms, rulers, and authorities in the unseen world. So, Lord, let Your kingdom be manifest on earth even as it is in heaven.

TUESDAY: YOUR WILL. Since everything was created through Christ and for Him let His will be done on earth as it is in heaven.

WEDNESDAY: GIVE US. Lord, You spoke and all that is came into existence. Just as You fed Your people manna in the desert, I have full trust that You will provide for me. Give me this day my daily bread.

THURSDAY: FORGIVE US. It was Your plan from before the beginning of time that Christ would be crucified. Father, thank You for redemption through the cross.

FRIDAY: LEAD US. As the architect of the universe, You know exactly my going out and my coming in. Guide me to be in perfect harmony with Your plan.

SATURDAY: DELIVER US. You were all wise in creating a plan for our deliverance, even from the foundation of the world. Let Your deliverance come to the ends of the earth.

Grace

THE IMAGE OF GOD: "And the Word was made flesh, and dwelt among us, (and we beheld his glory, the glory as of the only begotten of the Father,) full of grace and truth… And of his fullness have all we received, and grace for grace. For the law was given by Moses, but grace and truth came by Jesus Christ" (JN. 1:14, 16-17. KJV).

▪ "And he gives grace generously. As the Scriptures say, 'God opposes the proud but gives grace to the humble'" (JAM. 4:6).

▪ "But the God of all grace, who hath called us unto his eternal glory by Christ Jesus, after that ye have suffered a while, make you perfect, stablish, strengthen, settle you" (1 PET. 5:10. KJV).

— DO NOT TEMPT GOD —

THE COMMAND OF CHRIST: Jesus responded, "The Scriptures also say, 'You must not test the LORD your God'" (MATT. 4:7).

▪ "And remember, when you are being tempted, do not say, 'God is tempting me.' God is never tempted to do wrong, and he never tempts anyone else. Temptation comes f rom our own desires, which entice us and drag us away. These desires give birth to sinful actions. And when sin is allowed to grow, it gives birth to death" (JAM. 1:13-15).

▪ "Don't be misled—you cannot mock the justice of God. You will always harvest what you plant. Those who live only to satisfy their own sinful nature will harvest decay and death from that sinful nature. But those who live to please the Spirit will harvest everlasting life from the Spirit" (GAL. 6:7-8).

- "And God is able to make all grace abound toward you, that you, always having all sufficiency in all things, may have an abundance for every good work...And by their prayer for you, who long for you because of the exceeding grace of God in you" (2 Cor. 9:8, 14. NKJV).
- "God saved you by his grace when you believed. And you can't take credit for this; it is a gift from God. Salvation is not a reward for the good things we have done, so none of us can boast about it. For we are God's masterpiece. He has created us anew in Christ Jesus, so we can do the good things he planned for us long ago" (Eph. 2:8-10).

✓ ――― LIVING IN ALIGNMENT WITH THE GRACE OF GOD ―――

☐ What does it mean that salvation is by grace and not by works?
☐ Am I pursuing grace by looking to God's word daily?
☐ Am I resting in His redemption?
☐ How can I cultivate the grace of God in my life?
☐ Why and how do I resist the grace of God?
☐ What is grace?
☐ What is iniquity?
☐ What is the inner source of temptation in my life?

FAITH IN ACTION: GIVE A POCKET GUIDE

- Give a *Great With God Pocket Guide* away to someone who would appreciate it. Explain to them how you are using the pocket guide. Share the Faith In Action Assignments. Ask them to join you.

More ideas at GreatWithGod.com

APPEAL TO HEAVEN: Use the **Lord's Prayer Index** to acknowledge the image of God as gracious.

WISBIT TIP: Pray out loud even when praying alone.

SUNDAY: YOUR NAME. Oh, God of all grace, I thank You that in Your kingdom You desire for mercy to triumph over judgment.

MONDAY: YOUR KINGDOM. Lord of the harvest, grant power to Your servants to preach the gospel to all nations. Raise up missionaries to go to every nation in our generation.

TUESDAY: YOUR WILL. Father I am completely dependent upon You. Give me the desire and power to do Your will.

WEDNESDAY: GIVE US. Lord, give me this day the grace I need to fulfill all the good works You have assigned for me. Give me wisdom, favor and an understanding heart.

THURSDAY: FORGIVE US. Oh God, I don't deserve Your mercy, but would You forgive me? I am not worthy or qualified to receive Your power. Cleanse me from my willfulness and make me a servant unto honor.

FRIDAY: LEAD US. God of grace, if You lead me I will succeed. Go with me for I will not go without You. Father, be my leader; add Your mercy and grace to my ventures.

SATURDAY: DELIVER US. Lord, I can't break free from sin on my own power, for I am powerless to do so. Grant me a double portion of Your grace that I may live in Your freedom from the power of sin.

7

Order

The Image of God: "For God [who is the source of their prophesying] is not a God of confusion and disorder but of peace and order. As [is the practice] in all the churches of the saints (God's people)" (1 Cor. 14:33 amp).

▪ "'To whom will you compare me? Who is my equal?' asks the Holy one. Look up into the heavens. Who created all the stars? He brings them out like an army, one after another, calling each by its name. Because of his great power and incomparable strength, not a single one is missing"(Is. 40:25-26).

▪ "Then God said, 'Let lights appear in the sky to separate the day from the night. Let them be signs to mark the seasons, days, and years'" (Gen. 1:14-15).

▪ "But there is one thing I want you to know: The head of every man is Christ, the head of woman is man, and the head of Christ is God" (1 Cor. 11:3).

— SEEK FIRST THE KINGDOM —

The Command of Christ: "Seek the Kingdom of God above all else, and live righteously, and he will give you everything you need" (Matt. 6:33).

▪ "If you look for me wholeheartedly, you will find me" (Jer. 29:13).

▪ "I once thought these things were valuable, but now I consider them worthless because of what Christ has done. Yes, everything else is worthless when compared with the infinite value of knowing Christ Jesus my Lord. For his sake I have discarded everything else, counting it all as garbage, so that I could gain Christ" (Phil. 3:7-8).

- "For the Lord's sake, submit to all human authority—whether the king as head of state, or the officials he has appointed. For the king has sent them to punish those who do wrong and to honor those who do right" (1 PET. 2:13-14).
- "The eyes of the LORD search the whole earth in order to strengthen those whose hearts are fully committed to him. What a fool you have been! From now on you will be at war" (2 CHRON. 16:9).
- "But I will honor those who honor me, and I will despise those who think lightly of me" (1 SAM. 2:30).

✓ — LIVING IN ALIGNMENT WITH THE GOD OF ORDER —

☐ What does it mean to me to understand that God is orderly in His essence?
☐ How can I bring order out of the chaos in my life?
☐ Is my life characterized by disorder or order? What differences does it make?
☐ What if I ignore government laws and ordinances?
☐ What does it mean to seek God first?
☐ What would I have to change to put God first in my life?
☐ Is there any evidence that God is first in my life?

FAITH IN ACTION: 5 MOST WANTED

- Create a Top 5 list by writing the names of family, friends, or colleagues for you to pray that God would grant them eternal life. Use the space below.

1_____ 2_____ 3_____ 4_____ 5_____

More ideas at GreatWithGod.com

APPEAL TO HEAVEN: Use the **Lord's Prayer Index** to acknowledge that the nature of God is order.

SUNDAY: YOUR NAME. God, I thank You and praise You, for the heavens and the earth declare Your great glory. Your creation demonstrates Your perfect order; it is too marvelous for me to fully comprehend.

MONDAY: YOUR KINGDOM. May the eternal dimension of Your kingdom come. Let eternal life come to my family, friends, and colleagues (list specific names).

TUESDAY: YOUR WILL. Let everything done in the name of the Lord be decently and orderly, let it be so in our churches, families and schools.

WEDNESDAY: GIVE US. Lord, please grant me a wise and understanding heart that I might discern Your will and teach others Your ways.

THURSDAY: FORGIVE US. Dear God, have mercy upon me for the chaos I have created in my life through sloth and rebellion. Lord, I have rejected Your design in favor of my pleasure. I do not deserve Your forgiveness, but would You forgive me and renew a right spirit inside of me.

FRIDAY: LEAD US. Help me to discover Your principles and Your patterns that You have ordained that I may live in harmony with Your creation and Your design.

SATURDAY: DELIVER US. Lord, I am entrapped by my own doing. I ask You now to deliver me from my disorganized self. Deliver me from chaos and let Your order be manifested in every area of my life.

8

Judge

THE IMAGE OF GOD: "And I saw a great white throne and the one sitting on it. The earth and sky fled from his presence, but they found no place to hide. I saw the dead, both great and small, standing before God's throne. And the books were opened, including the Book of Life. And the dead were judged according to what they had done, as recorded in the books" (REV. 20:11-12).

▪ "But those who wish to boast should boast in this alone: that they truly know me and understand that I am the Lord who demonstrates unfailing love and who brings justice and righteousness to the earth, and that I delight in these things. I, the Lord, have spoken!" (JER. 9:24).

▪ "Nothing in all creation is hidden from God. Everything is naked and exposed before his eyes, and he is the one to whom we are accountable" (HEB. 4:13).

— JUDGE NOT —

THE COMMAND OF CHRIST: "Do not judge others, and you will not be judged. For you will be treated as you treat others. The standard you use in judging is the standard by which you will be judged" (MATT. 7:1-2).

▪ "Don't speak evil against each other, dear brothers and sisters. If you criticize and judge each other, then you are criticizing and judging God's law. But your job is to obey the law, not to judge whether it applies to you. God alone, who gave the law, is the Judge" (JAM. 4:11-12).

▪ "When you say they are wicked and should be punished, you are condemning yourself, for you who judge others do these very same things" (ROM. 2:1).

- "There will be no mercy for those who have not shown mercy to others. But if you have been merciful, God will be merciful when he judges you" (JAM. 2:13).
- "For we must all stand before Christ to be judged. We will each receive whatever we deserve for the good or evil we have done in this earthly body" (2 COR. 5:10).
- "Then he added, "Now go and learn the meaning of this Scripture: 'I want you to show mercy, not offer sacrifices.' For I have come to call not those who think they are righteous, but those who know they are sinners" (MATT. 9:13).

✓ —— LIVING IN ALIGNMENT WITH THE JUDGE OF ALL THINGS ——

☐ What qualities does God uniquely possess that qualify Him to be my judge?

☐ Am I prepared to stand before the judgment seat of Christ? What will I be held accountable for?

☐ How will it affect my life on earth if I ignore the truth that I will one day be held accountable for all my deeds?

☐ Do I lean more towards mercy or towards judgment?

☐ When I correct someone do I check myself to see if I have the same fault?

FAITH IN ACTION: PRAY FOR LEADERS

- Don't be an accuser; be an intercessor.

- Pray for our nation's leaders: president, judges, mayors, governors. Research and write their names in this book. Ask God to bless them with a spirit of wisdom and understanding, to protect them, and give them a saving knowledge of Jesus Christ.

More ideas at GreatWithGod.com

APPEAL TO HEAVEN: Use the **Lord's Prayer Index** to acknowledge God as perfectly just.

SUNDAY: YOUR NAME. I praise You, Lord, for You alone are all wise and all knowing. You alone are perfect and therefore the only being in the universe capable of rendering justice.

MONDAY: YOUR KINGDOM. Lord God, I want You to be the judge over all. I want Your rule and Your rules to govern the life of all people. Let Your justice be established in our land and in our courts.

TUESDAY: YOUR WILL. Judge of all, let Your righteous verdicts reign on the earth. Raise up Your leaders to uphold Your righteous decrees. Change the hearts and minds of those in authority who oppose Your righteousness.

WEDNESDAY: GIVE US. Lord God, give me patience with sinful people, for I myself once lived in rebellion against You. Incline my heart to Your word that I might desire to walk in Your path of truth.

THURSDAY: FORGIVE US. Lord, I have failed to live up to Your righteous standards; have mercy on me. I humbly ask that the payment Christ made for my forgiveness be remembered and that You would cleanse me from all unrighteousness.

FRIDAY: LEAD US. Father, raise up government leaders and leaders in our churches who will lead us in the path of righteousness.

SATURDAY: DELIVER US. Oh God, deliver us from those rulers on earth who promote evil. Remove the wicked from authority. Deliver me, I pray, from evil.

Eternal

THE IMAGE OF GOD: "From eternity to eternity I am God. No one can snatch anyone out of My hand. No one can undo what I have done" (Is. 43:13).

• "In the beginning the Word already existed. The Word was with God, and the Word was God. He existed in the beginning with God. God created everything through Him, and nothing was created except through Him. The Word gave life to everything that was created, and His life brought light to everyone" (Jn. 1:1-4).

• "Yet God has made everything beautiful for its own time. He has planted eternity in the human heart, but even so, people cannot see the whole scope of God's work from beginning to end" (Eccl. 3:11).

— AWAIT MY RETURN —

THE COMMAND OF CHRIST: "So you, too, must keep watch! For you don't know what day your Lord is coming. Understand this: If a homeowner knew exactly when a burglar was coming, he would keep watch and not permit his house to be broken into. You also must be ready all the time, for the Son of Man will come when least expected" (Matt. 24:42-44).

• "Dear friends, we are already God's children, but he has not yet shown us what we will be like when Christ appears. But we do know that we will be like him, for we will see him as he really is" (1 Jn. 3:2).

• "The end of the world is coming soon. Therefore, be earnest and disciplined in your prayers" (1 Pet. 4:7).

• "Look, I am coming soon, bringing my reward with me to repay all people according to their deeds" (Rev. 22:12).

▪ "And anyone who believes in God's Son has eternal life. Anyone who doesn't obey the Son will never experience eternal life but remains under God's angry judgment" (Jn. 3:36).

▪ "They know the truth about God because he has made it obvious to them. For ever since the world was created, people have seen the earth and sky. Through everything God made, they can clearly see his invisible qualities—his eternal power and divine nature. So they have no excuse for not knowing God" (Rom. 1:19-20).

▪ "I have written this to you who believe in the name of the Son of God, so that you may know you have eternal life" (1 Jn. 5:13).

✓   — LIVING IN ALIGNMENT WITH THE ETERNAL GOD —

☐   Try to define what it means that God is eternal.

☐   What must I do to obtain eternal life?

☐   What if I ignore that God is at all places at all times?

☐   Can I have faith in God knowing that I will never fully understand the complete nature of God?

☐   What is a wrong perspective on awaiting Christ's return?

☐   What can I do to prepare for Christ's return?

☐   What signs should we look for that indicate the soon return of Christ?

FAITH IN ACTION: BLESS A PET OWNER

▪ Waiting on the Lord's return is a lot like a dog waiting for his master to come home. With that in mind, bless the owner of a pet with a gift for their furry friend. Say, "Here is a surprise gift for your pet. When Christ returns, He's also bringing gifts with Him."

More ideas at GreatWithGod.com

APPEAL TO HEAVEN: Use the **Lord's Prayer Index** to acknowledge the image of God as eternal.

SUNDAY: YOUR NAME. Praise the name of the Lord, and join with angels in proclaiming eternally, holy, holy, holy, is the Lord God Almighty.

MONDAY: YOUR KINGDOM. Oh Lord, may Your eternal attribute drive people to You. Let Your kingdom come in this age of the earth. And yet I await the manifestation of Your eternal kingdom. My heart eagerly awaits Your return.

TUESDAY: YOUR WILL. Your righteous right way of living never changes. Let Your unchanging eternal truth be established in our laws, in our churches, families, schools. If there are institutional laws and rules that are being reviewed at this moment, pray that God's way will prevail.)

WEDNESDAY: GIVE US. You are my faithful provider. Forever my eyes are upon You as my source for all things Your word feeds my soul and spirit.

THURSDAY: FORGIVE US. Lord, if I confess my sins (list Your specific sins) You promise to be faithful and just to forgive me my sins and the blood of Jesus Christ continually cleanses me from all my sins.

FRIDAY: LEAD US. Lord God, I am looking to You for direction in my life. Please guide me by opening doors no man can close, and help me remember that closed doors are also part of Your perfect plan.

SATURDAY: DELIVER US. Your word declares that all authority in heaven and earth belongs to the Lord Jesus Christ. Deliver me this day from evil.

GOD THE FATHER

THE JEHOVAH "I AM" NAMES OF GOD

10 JEHOVAH M'KADESH   THE LORD WHO SANCTIFIES YOU
11 JEHOVAH RAPHE   THE LORD WHO HEALS YOU
12 JEHOVAH SHAMMAH   THE LORD IS THERE
13 JEHOVAH NISSI   THE LORD IS MY BANNER
14 JEHOVAH JIREH   THE LORD IS MY PROVIDER
15 YAHWEH   ADONI I AM – THE LORD

PRAY USING THE TABERNACLE PRAYER INDEX

YOUR GOAL: PRAY THROUGH THE TABERNACLE PRAYER EACH DAY, AND THEN PRAY FOR 5 MINUTES CONCERNING THE INDEX THEME ASSIGNED EACH DAY. USE THE PRAYER GUIDE AT THE END OF EACH CHAPTER TO HELP YOU GET STARTED.

ON SATURDAY, COMPLETE YOUR MEDITATION FOR THE WEEK BY PRAYING COMPLETELY THROUGH THE PRAYER WHEEL INDEX IN 35 MINUTES.

WISBIT TIP: BECAUSE THE BLOOD SACRIFICE OF JESUS CHRIST CONTINUALLY CLEANSES YOU FROM YOU SIN, YOU MAY COME BOLDLY AND CONFIDENTLY INTO GOD'S PRESENCE . (SEE EPH. 3:12)

TABERNACLE PRAYER INDEX

Lord, as I pray through the tabernacle, I come to the **Outer Courts,** and present my body to You. Then, I come to the **Brazen Alter,** mindful that Christ was sacrificed as my substitute. He took my sin and gave me His righteousness. The **Laver** is my bathing mirror reminding me to examine myself and so purify myself to Your holy standards. The **Candlestick** reminds me to pray, "Holy Spirit lets go together throughout this day." The **Show Bread** is the word of God and reminds me that man does not live by bread alone but rather by every word that proceeds from the mouth of God. The **Alter of Incense** reminds me to pray for others. And when I enter the holy of holies, I am comforted by Your **Mercy Seat.** For Your desire for mercy is greater than Your desire for judgment. Amen.

Tabernacle Furniture Prayer Index

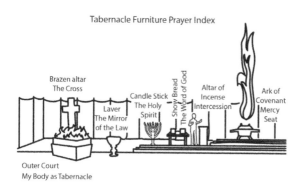

Inspiration for the Tabernacle Index from Dr. David Yonggi Cho. Learn how to pray Tabernacle Prayer.[3]

Jehovah M'kadesh
(THE LORD WHO SANCTIFIES ME)

THE IMAGE OF GOD: "Consecrate yourselves therefore, and be holy, for I am the Lord your God. And you shall keep My statutes, and perform them: I am the Lord who sanctifies you (Jehovah M'Kadesh)" (LEV. 20:7-8).

▪ "And the Lord spoke to Moses, saying, 'Speak also to the children of Israel, saying: "Surely My Sabbaths you shall keep, for it is a sign between Me and you throughout your generations that you may know that I am the Lord who sanctifies you"''" (EX. 31:12-13).

▪ "And all who have this eager expectation will keep themselves pure, just as he is pure" (1 JN. 3:3).

▪ "For this is the will of God, your sanctification: that you should abstain from sexual immorality; that each of you should know how to possess his own vessel in sanctification and honor, not in passion of lust, like the Gentiles who do not know God" (1 THES. 4:3-5).

⸺ BAPTIZE MY DISCIPLES ⸺

THE COMMAND OF CHRIST: "Therefore, go and make disciples of all the nations, baptizing them in the name of the Father and the Son and the Holy Spirit" (MATT. 28:19).

▪ "For there is one body and one Spirit, just as you have been called to one glorious hope for the future. There is one Lord, one faith, one baptism, one God and Father of all, who is over all, in all, and living through all" (EPH. 4:4-6).

▪ "Peter replied, 'Each of you must repent of your sins and turn to God, and be baptized in the name of Jesus Christ for the forgiveness of your sins. Then you will receive the gift of the Holy Spirit'" (ACTS 2:38).

▪ "Now may the God of peace Himself sanctify you completely; and may your whole spirit, soul, and body be preserved blameless at the coming of our Lord Jesus Christ. He who calls you is faithful who also will do it" (1 THES. 5:23-24).

▪ "Make them holy by your truth; teach them your word, which is truth" (JN. 17:17).

▪ "And I give myself as a holy sacrifice for them so they can be made holy by your truth" (JN. 17:19).

▪ "But if we confess our sins to him, he is faithful and just to forgive us our sins and to cleanse us from all wickedness" (1 JN. 1:9).

— LIVING IN ALIGNMENT WITH THE GOD WHO SANCTIFIES —

☐ What does it mean: the Lord who Sanctifies me?
☐ How can I sanctify myself? Do I need to repent?
☐ How do the Scriptures sanctify a person?
☐ What difference does it make if I'm baptized or not?
☐ What are the various tools God uses to sanctify me?
☐ How can I cooperate with God in His work to sanctify me? Can I resist it?
☐ Who should be baptized?
☐ What does it mean to be baptized?

FAITH IN ACTION: BAPTISM

▪ Have you been baptized? Would you like to be baptized? If you'd like to be baptized, make arrangements to do so this week or assist a friend to be baptized.

More ideas at GreatWithGod.com

APPEAL TO HEAVEN: Use the **Tabernacle Index** to acknowledge the image of God as sanctifier.

SUNDAY: OUTER COURT. MY BODY AS TABERNACLE. Lord God, I present the members of my body to You as a living sacrifice. I give You my hands to do as You direct. I give You my feet to go where You desire. Live through me. Make me a channel of Your sanctification.

MONDAY: BRAZEN ALTER. THE CROSS. I am sanctified and made holy by the blood of Jesus Christ. By Your blood all my sins are washed away. I am clean by the Blood of the Lamb.

TUESDAY: LAVER. THE MIRROR OF THE LAW. Lord, I have looked into Your perfect Law and confess that I have not loved You with all my heart and I have made idols of so many of my possessions. Sanctify me with Your truth.

WEDNESDAY: CANDLE STICK. THE HOLY SPIRIT. Holy Spirit, come and convict me of any sin that stands between us. Give me the power this day to live a holy life.

THURSDAY: SHOW BREAD. THE WORD OF GOD. Your words, oh Lord, are the source of my sanctification. Help me to hide Your word in my heart that I might not sin against You.

FRIDAY: ALTER OF INCENSE. INTERCESSION. You are coming for Your bride (the church) and she is to be without spot or wrinkle. Do whatever it takes to make Your church holy.

SATURDAY: ARK OF COVENANT. MERCY SEAT. Let Your unfailing mercy come to the ends of the earth. First come to my city. Raise up laborers to work in my city. Raise up holy leaders who will lead holy ministries.

Jehovah Rapha
(THE LORD IS MY HEALER)

THE IMAGE OF GOD: "And said, "If you diligently heed the voice of the Lord your God and do what is right in His sight, give ear to His commandments and keep all His statutes, I will put none of the diseases on you which I have brought on the Egyptians. For I am the Lord who heals you (Jehovah Rapha)" (Ex. 15:26).

▪ "Surely He has borne our griefs and carried our sorrows; yet we esteemed Him stricken, smitten by God, and afflicted. But He was wounded for our transgressions, He was bruised for our iniquities, the chastisement for our peace was upon Him, and by His stripes we are healed" (ISA. 53:4-5).

▪ "Jesus traveled throughout the region of Galilee, teaching in the synagogues and announcing the Good News about the Kingdom. And he healed every kind of disease and illness" (MATT. 4:23).

—— FORGIVE OFFENDERS ——

THE COMMAND OF CHRIST: "Then Peter came to him and asked, 'Lord, how often should I forgive someone who sins against me? Seven times?' 'No, not seven times,' Jesus replied, 'but seventy times seven!'" (Matt. 18:21-22).

▪ "If you forgive those who sin against you, your heavenly Father will forgive you. But if you refuse to forgive others, your Father will not forgive your sins" (Matt. 6:15).

▪ "Make allowance for each other's faults, and forgive anyone who offends you. Remember, the Lord forgave you, so you must forgive others" (Col. 3:12-13).

• "Are any of you sick? You should call for the elders of the church to come and pray over you, anointing you with oil in the name of the Lord" (JAM. 5:14.).

• "If My people who are called by My name will humble themselves, and pray and seek My face, and turn from their wicked ways, then I will hear from heaven, and will forgive their sin and heal their land" (2 CHRON. 7:14).

✓   —— LIVING IN ALIGNMENT WITH THE GOD WHO HEALS ——

☐ What does it mean that the Lord is my healer?

☐ Why doesn't God answer every prayer for healing with immediate manifestation?

☐ How can I know if I have unforgiveness in my heart?

☐ Does my forgiveness have limits?

☐ What are the consequences of unforgiveness?

☐ What's more important: healing the body or the soul?

☐ When the Scriptures say "By His stripes we are healed," what does that mean?

☐ What is the purpose for God allowing sickness?

☐ What are the various ways that God heals people?

☐ Do I understand the dynamic relationship that exists between sickness of the soul and sickness in the body?

FAITH IN ACTION: PRAY FOR HEALING

• Pray for God to use you as a channel of His healing power. Stay alert for the opportunity to offer prayer for the recovery of the sick and possibly use anointing oil as you pray for the sick. Stay attuned and be ready to pray for those who are in emotional pain.

More ideas at GreatWithGod.com

Appeal to Heaven: Use the **Tabernacle Index** to acknowledge the image of God as my healer.

Sunday: Outer Court. My Body as Tabernacle: Lord God my healer, I present my body to You as a living sacrifice. Give me the exact health I need to fulfill all the good works You have assigned for me to do.

Monday: Brazen Alter. The Cross: I thank You that through the blood of Jesus Christ, by His stripes, I am healed. Jehovah Rapha, come heal me.

Tuesday: Laver. The Mirror of the Law: Lord, look and see if there is any evil way in me. Heal my heart and my mind as I seek to obey Your commandments.

Wednesday: Candle Stick. The Holy Spirit: Holy Spirit, come now and be my comforter in time of tribulation. It is the manifestation of the gift of the Holy Spirit that is healing. Let Your healing come now.

Thursday: Show Bread. The Word of God: It is written in Your word that the spirit of the Lord shall come upon the Messiah to bind up the broken-hearted and give sight to the blind. Lord, send forth Your word and heal Your people.

Friday: Alter of Incense. Intercession: Lord, I stand in a place of intercession, asking now for Your healing to come to those in my sphere of influence who need Your healing touch. Intercede for ill friends and family.

Saturday: Ark of Covenant. Mercy Seat: Lord, let Your healing salvation come to lost souls in this generation. Raise up laborers to go on Your behalf and bring Your healing power to the ends of the earth.

12 *Jehovah Shamma*
(THE LORD IS THERE)

THE IMAGE OF GOD: "'Behold, I am with you and will keep you wherever you go, and will bring you back to this land; for I will not leave you until I have done what I have spoken to you.' Then Jacob awoke f rom his sleep and said, 'Surely the Lord is in this place, (Jehovah Shamma), and I did not know it.' And he was af raid and said, 'How awesome is this place! This is none other than the house of God, and this is the gate of heaven!'" (GEN. 28:15-17).

▪ "All the way around shall be eighteen thousand cubits (6 miles); and the name of the city from that day shall be; THE LORD IS THERE!" (EZEK. 48:35).

▪ "And she will have a son, and you are to name him Jesus, for he will save his people from their sins." All of this occurred to fulfill the Lord's message through his prophet: Look! The virgin will conceive a child! She will give birth to a son, and they will call him Emmanuel, which means 'God is with us'" (MATT. 1:21-23).

— BE A HOUSE OF PRAYER —

THE COMMAND OF CHRIST: "He said to them, 'The Scriptures declare, "My Temple will be called a house of prayer for all nations," but you have turned it into a den of thieves!'" (MARK 11:17).

▪ "Don't you realize that all of you together are the temple of God and that the Spirit of God lives in you?" (1 COR. 3:16-17).

▪ "I will bring them to my holy mountain of Jerusalem and will fill them with joy in my house of prayer. I will accept their burnt offerings and sacrifices, because my Temple will be called a House of Prayer for all nations" (IS. 56:7).

- "I will live among you, and I will not despise you. I will walk among you; I will be your God, and you will be My people" (Lev. 26:11-12).
- "When you go out to fight your enemies…Do not lose heart or panic or tremble before them. For the Lord your God is going with you! He will fight for you against your enemies, and He will give you victory!" (Deut. 20:1-4).
- "For where two or three gather as my followers, I am there among them" (Matt. 18:20).
- "I can never escape from your Spirit! I can never get away from your presence! If I go up to heaven, you are there; if I go down to the grave, you are there" (Ps. 139:7-8).

✓   —– LIVING IN ALIGNMENT WITH THE OMNIPRESENT GOD —–

☐ What does it mean to me to know that He will never leave me nor forsake me even until the end of this age?
☐ Am I continuously aware that God is watching me and completely aware of my every thought, word and deed.
☐ Is there a special place I go to enjoy presence of the Lord?
☐ What makes a place sacred to the Lord?
☐ Are there blessings in my life that can only be explained by His presence in my life?

FAITH IN ACTION: BE A HOUSE OF PRAYER

- Honor the sabbath. Go to church. Pray a special prayer that your church would become a house of prayer. Ask God to increase the prayer ministry at your church. Honoring the sabbath is an all-day affair. Spend the afternoon praying and reading the scriptures.

More ideas at GreatWithGod.com

APPEAL TO HEAVEN: Use the **Tabernacle Index** to acknowledge the image of God as always with me.

SUNDAY: OUTER COURT. MY BODY AS TABERNACLE. Lord, I give You my eyes; let me see the world the way You see the world. I give You my ears; let me hear the world the way You hear it.. Make me an expression of Your presence.

MONDAY: BRAZEN ALTER. THE CROSS. You, oh Lord, have exchanged my sin for Christ's righteousness, therefore I am righteous by the Blood of the Lamb.

TUESDAY: LAVER. THE MIRROR OF THE LAW. Lord, I looked into Your perfect Law and confess that I have taken Your name in vain and I have cursed others; profanity is in my heart and in my mouth. Lord, I repent; wash and cleanse me.

WEDNESDAY: CANDLE STICK. THE HOLY SPIRIT. I am to seek first Your kingdom and Your right way of living. It is my desire to seek You first. Holy Spirit, as I seek You please make Yourself easily found.

THURSDAY: SHOW BREAD. THE WORD OF GOD. Your words, oh Lord, are found in the Holy Bible. I purpose now to keep Your commands ever before my eyes.

FRIDAY: ALTER OF INCENSE. INTERCESSION. Oh Lord, You said seek my face, and Your face, Oh Lord, I have sought .Have mercy on my family; turn their hearts to You as well.

SATURDAY: ARK OF COVENANT. MERCY SEAT. Raise up ministries in my state who will defend the widow and the orphan, who will feed the poor and comfort the homeless. Be present and let Your name be famous in my state. Cause this state to shine brightly forth to the ends of the earth.

Jehovah Nissi
(THE LORD IS MY BANNER)

THE IMAGE OF GOD: "So Joshua defeated Amalek and his people with the edge of the sword. Then the Lord said to Moses, 'Write this for a memorial in the book and recount it in the hearing of Joshua that I will utterly blot out the remembrance of Amalek f rom under heaven.' And Moses built an altar and called its name, The-Lord-Is-My-Banner (Jehovah Nissi)" (Ex. 17:13-15).

▪ "(Elijah said), 'Hear me, O LORD, hear me, that this people may know that You are the LORD God, and that You have turned their hearts back to You again.' Then the fire of the Lord fell and consumed the burnt sacrifice, and the wood and the stones and the dust, and it licked up the water that was in the trench" (1 KINGS 18:37-38).

— BEWARE OF FALSE PROPHETS —

THE COMMAND OF CHRIST: "Beware of false prophets who come disguised as harmless sheep but are really vicious wolves. You can identify them by their fruit, that is, by the way they act. Can you pick grapes from thorn bushes, or figs from thistles? A good tree produces good fruit, and a bad tree produces bad fruit. A good tree can't produce bad fruit, and a bad tree can't produce good fruit. So every tree that does not produce good fruit is chopped down and thrown into the fire. Yes, just as you can identify a tree by its fruit, so you can identify people by their actions" (MATT. 7:15-20).

▪ "These people are false apostles. They are deceitful workers who disguise themselves as apostles of Christ. But I am not surprised! Even Satan disguises himself as an angel of light" (2 COR. 11:13-14).

• "Teach these new disciples to obey all the commands I have given you. And be sure of this: I am with you always, even to the end of the age" (MATT. 28:20).

• "No one will be able to stand against you as long as you live. For I will be with you as I was with Moses. I will not fail you or abandon you" (JOSH. 1:5).

✓   —— LIVING IN ALIGNMENT WITH THE LORD MY BANNER ——

☐ When God reveals Himself as the Lord my Banner, what does that communicate to me?

☐ What difference does it make to my faith to understand the Lord is my Banner?

☐ When I identify myself as a Christian is that the same as saying the Lord is my Banner?

☐ To pray in the name of Jesus is that a fulfillment of the Lord is my Banner?

☐ If Satan is able to disguise himself as an angel of light how will I be able uncover his charade?

☐ Has the Lord sent a message to me calling me to return to Him?

☐ Do I have any reminders of what miracles God has done for me in the past?

FAITH IN ACTION: HOME JERICHO PRAYER WALK

• Pray as you walk around the outside perimeter of your home. And then pray as you intentionally walk through the various rooms of your house. Pray for the needs of the people who live in those rooms. Use the function (activities) of each room as prayer index.

More ideas at GreatWithGod.com

Appeal to Heaven: Use the **Tabernacle** index to acknowledge that I represent God's name to this world.

Sunday: Outer Court. My Body as Tabernacle. Lord God, my body is Your temple. I am Your child and I bear Your name. You and I are one. I choose today to identify with You and Your kingdom. I will be Your ambassador.

Monday: Brazen Alter. The Cross. Jesus, through Your blood and Your death on the cross You have conquered the world and the devil so that I might be cleansed from all my sins.

Tuesday: Laver. The Mirror of the Law. Lord, hatred is the same as murder and lust is the same as adultery. Forgive me for have I sinned in thought, word and deed. Renew a right spirit in me.

Wednesday: Candle Stick. The Holy Spirit. Holy Spirit, Your banner over me is love. I follow You and I will not follow any other. Deliver me from false prophets and give me a discerning spirit so I can know the difference.

Thursday: Show Bread. The Word of God. Your word is truth sharper than any two-edged sword piercing between soul and spirit. Teach me Your word so I can learn to discern what is false and what is true.

Friday: Alter of Incense. Intercession. Oh Lord, You have won the victory and all authority in heaven and earth belongs to You. I pray that You would send me forth to make disciples of all the nations. I will go in Your victory.

Saturday: Ark of Covenant. Mercy Seat. Lord, I take comfort that You will never leave me or forsake me to the end of the age. Holy Spirit, let's go together to all the nations. You be the leader and I will follow.

14 *Jehovah Jireh*
(THE LORD IS MY PROVIDER)

THE IMAGE OF GOD: "Then Abraham lifted his eyes and looked, and there behind him was a ram caught in a thicket by its horns. So Abraham went and took the ram, and offered it up for a burnt offering instead of his son. And Abraham called the name of the place, The-Lord-Will-Provide, (Jehovah Jireh), as it is said to this day, "In the Mount of the Lord it shall be provided" (GEN. 22:13-14).

▪ "Look at the birds of the air, for they neither sow nor reap nor gather into barns, yet your heavenly Father feeds them. Are you not of more value than they?" (MATT. 6:26).

▪ "And my God shall supply all your need according to His riches in glory by Christ Jesus" (PHIL. 4:19).

— ASK, SEEK, AND KNOCK —

THE COMMAND OF CHRIST: "Keep on asking, and you will receive what you ask for. Keep on seeking, and you will find. Keep on knocking, and the door will be opened to you. For everyone who asks, receives. Everyone who seeks, finds. And to everyone who knocks, the door will be opened" (MATT. 7:7-8).

▪ "You parents: If your children ask for a loaf of bread, do you give them a stone instead? So, if you sinful people know how to give good gifts to your children, how much more will your heavenly Father give good gifts to those who ask him."

▪ "It is the father's good pleasure to give you the kingdom" (MATT. 7:9, 11).

▪ "Yes, ask me for anything in my name, and I will do it!" (JN. 14:14).

▪ "Seek the Kingdom of God above all else, and live righteously, and he will give you everything you need" (MATT. 6:33).

▪ "I love all who love me. Those who search will surely find me" (PROV. 8:17).

▪ "Yet you don't have what you want because you don't ask God for it. And even when you ask, you don't get it because your motives are all wrong—you want only what will give you pleasure" (JAM. 4:2-3).

✓ ── LIVING IN ALIGNMENT WITH THE GOD WHO PROVIDES ──

☐ What does it mean to me that the Lord is my provider?

☐ Who do I go to first to fulfill my needs?

☐ What's the difference between asking, seeking, and knocking?

☐ When have I persisted in praying for Gods provision?

☐ Has God ever provided for a need after prayer? When?

☐ What does it mean when God doesn't supply my need as I requested?

☐ What else can God provide for me besides money?

FAITH IN ACTION: THE GIVING POCKET[4]

▪ Set apart from your money $5-$20. Dedicate this to God. It is no longer yours. But see yourself as God's delivery agent. Carry the money with you, be ready and prepared to distribute. Ask God to show you who He'd like you to give this to. As you give it, say, "I have a delivery for you, this is a gift from God. I'm merely His delivery agent. He is your provider. He wants you to know that He sees you and he cares for you.

More ideas at GreatWithGod.com

Appeal to Heaven: Use the **Tabernacle Index** to acknowledge the image of God as provider.

Sunday: Outer Court. My Body as Tabernacle. Lord God, I present the members of my body to You as a living sacrifice. I give You my mouth that I may speak Your words. Give me boldness and courage to speak the truth in love.

Monday: Brazen Alter. The Cross. I am blessed because of the cross, for it is written cursed is everyone who hangeth on a tree. A great exchange happened at the cross, all of the punishment that was due me was put on Christ and the righteousness of Christ was put on me. Now all the blessings of keeping the law are upon me.

Tuesday: Laver. The Mirror of the Law. Lord, I have not honored the Sabbath nor have I always honored my parents. Forgive me and give me strength to keep these commandments.

Wednesday: Candle stick. The Holy Spirit. Lord, You said to ask and to seek and to knock persistently in prayer. I am desperate for You; hear my cry now. Jehovah Jireh, provide for my needs or I perish.

Thursday: Show Bread. The Word of God. I do not live by bread alone but by every word that proceeds from the mouth of God. Provide insight to the meaning of Your words for me today.

Friday: Alter of Incense. Intercession. Oh Lord, provide for and defend Your church and her leaders.

Saturday: Ark of Covenant. Mercy Seat. Let Your gospel be preached throughout my country. Lord, provide pastors, evangelist, apostles and prophets to speak truth and care for Your people. Raise them up, I pray.

Yahweh
(I AM)

The Image of God: "But Moses protested, 'If I go to the people of Israel and tell them, "The God of your ancestors has sent me to you," they will ask me, "What is his name?" Then what should I tell them?' God replied to Moses, 'I AM who I AM. Say this to the people of Israel: I AM (Yahweh) has sent me to you.' God also said to Moses, 'Say this to the people of Israel: Yahweh, the God of your ancestors—the God of Abraham, the God of Isaac, and the God of Jacob—has sent me to you. This is my eternal name, my name to remember for all generations'" (Ex. 3:13-15).

▪ "I am the Alpha and the Omega—the beginning and the end," says the Lord God. "I am the one who is, who always was, and who is still to come—the Almighty One" (Rev. 1:8).

— LAY UP TREASURE —

The Command of Christ: "Don't store up treasures here on earth, where moths eat them and rust destroys them, and where thieves break in and steal. Store your treasures in heaven, where moths and rust cannot destroy, and thieves do not break in and steal. Wherever your treasure is, there the desires of your heart will also be" (Matt. 6:19-21).

▪ "And if you are untrustworthy about worldly wealth, who will trust you with the true riches of heaven?" (Luke 16:11).

▪ "When Jesus heard his answer, he said, 'There is still one thing you haven't done. Sell all your possessions and give the money to the poor, and you will have treasure in heaven. Then come, follow me'" (Luke 18:22).

- "He replied, 'What is impossible for people is possible with God'" (LUKE 18:27).
- "Jesus looked at them intently and said, 'Humanly speaking, it is impossible. But with God everything is possible'" (MATT. 19:26).
- "For I can do everything through Christ, who gives me strength" (PHIL. 4:13).
- "I am the LORD, the God of all the peoples of the world. Is anything too hard for me?" (JER. 32:27).

✓   — LIVING IN ALIGNMENT WITH THE GREAT I AM —

☐ Am I at peace with the fact that I will never fully understand the eternal dimension of God in this lifetime?

☐ Do I take comfort in the eternal dimension of God?

☐ Since God really exists, how should I adjust my life to this fact?

☐ Do I understand why I was created?

☐ How can I become best friends with God?

☐ If God is for me who can be against me?

☐ Is there anything God cannot do?

☐ Do I acknowledge and worship God for who He is?

FAITH IN ACTION: LAY UP TREASURE

- Give to a Christian charity/ministry of your choice. The idea is to follow Christ's command to lay up treasure in heaven. Make a practical impact by participating monetarily in bringing His kingdom reign to earth. Give to ministry done in Jesus' name.

More ideas at GreatWithGod.com

Appeal to Heaven: Use the **Tabernacle Index** to acknowledge the image of God as **I AM**.

Sunday: Outer Court. My Body as Tabernacle. Lord, I present my body to You as a living sacrifice. You died that I might live, so now I give my life to You. This is a reasonable exchange.

Monday: Brazen Alter. The Cross. Lord Jesus, through Your blood I have been redeemed from death and hell. I am resurrected with You and in the Spirit I am seated with You right now at the right hand of God.

Tuesday: Laver. The Mirror of the Law. Lord, I am convicted of the things I have done. I have lied, I have stolen and I have coveted. Lord, have mercy upon me; grant me to walk in truth, generosity and contentment.

Wednesday: Candle Stick. The Holy Spirit. Holy Spirit, You are joined to me as a man is joined to His wife. You be the senior partner; I will be the junior.

Thursday: Show Bread. The Word of God. Oh, how I love Your truth! It is my meditation all the day. You have made me wiser than my teachers, for Your commandments are ever before me.

Friday: Alter of Incense. Intercession. Oh Lord, You have won the victory. All authority in heaven and earth belongs to You. You said to Your Son, "Only ask, and I will give the nations as Your inheritance." I ask for the salvation of all nations.

Saturday: Ark of Covenant. Mercy Seat. Lord, you are my all in all. I declare that there is no other name upon earth by which men must be saved, that at the name of Jesus every knee shall bow and every tongue confess. He is Lord.

GOD THE SON

JESUS IMAGE

PRAY USING THE HIGH PRIESTLY BLESSINGS FAN

YOUR GOAL: PRAY THROUGH THE HIGH PRIESTLY BLESSING EACH DAY. THEN PRAY FOR 5 MINUTES CONCERNING THE INDEX THEME ASSIGNED EACH DAY. USE THE PRAYER GUIDE AT THE END OF EACH CHAPTER TO HELP YOU GET STARTED.

ON SATURDAY, COMPLETE YOUR MEDITATION FOR THE WEEK BY PRAYING COMPLETELY THROUGH THE PRAYER WHEEL INDEX IN 35 MINUTES.

WISBIT TIP: MEMORIZE AND OFFER THIS HIGH PRIESTLY BLESSING AS A CLOSING PRAYER AT YOUR NEXT STUDY OR FELLOWSHIP GATHERING.

THE HIGH PRIESTLY BLESSING INDEX

"Then the Lord said to Moses, 'Tell Aaron and his sons to bless the people of Israel with this special blessing: May the Lord bless you and protect you. May the Lord smile on you and be gracious to you. May the Lord show you his favor and give you his peace. Whenever Aaron and his sons bless the people of Israel in my name, I myself will bless them'" (Numbers 6:22-27).

Coupled with the Blessing of Abraham, "I will make you into a great nation. I will bless you and make you famous, and you will be a blessing to others" (Gen. 12:2).

High Priest Blessing Index Fan

16 the Word Made Flesh
"THE RABBI"

THE IMAGE OF GOD: "And the Word was made flesh, and dwelt among us, (and we beheld his glory, the glory as of the only begotten of the Father) full of grace and truth" (JN. 1:14 KJV).

▪ "In the beginning the Word already existed. The Word was with God, and the Word was God. He existed in the beginning with God. God created everything through him, and nothing was created except through him. The Word gave life to everything that was created, and his life brought light to everyone" (JN. 1:1-4).

▪ "Christ is the visible image of the invisible God. He existed before anything was created and is supreme over all creation, for through him God created everything in the heavenly realms and on earth. He made the things we can see and the things we can't see—such as thrones, kingdoms, rulers, and authorities in the unseen world. Everything was created through him and for him" (COL. 1:15-16).

—— TAKE, EAT, DRINK ——

THE COMMAND OF CHRIST: "As they were eating, Jesus took some bread and blessed it. Then he broke it in pieces and gave it to the disciples, saying, 'Take this and eat it, for this is my body.' And he took a cup of wine and gave thanks to God for it. He gave it to them and said, 'Each of you drink from it'" (MATT. 26:26-27).

▪ "After supper he took another cup of wine and said, 'This cup is the new covenant between God and his people—an agreement confirmed with my blood, which is poured out as a sacrifice for you'" (LUKE 22:20).

• "That is why you should examine yourself before eating the bread and drinking the cup. For if you eat the bread or drink the cup without honoring the body of Christ, you are eating and drinking God's judgment upon yourself. That is why many of you are weak and sick and some have even died" (1 COR. 11:28-30).

"In the same way, he took the cup of wine after supper, saying, 'This cup is the new covenant between God and his people—an agreement confirmed with my blood. Do this in remembrance of me as often as you drink it.' For every time you eat this bread and drink this cup, you are announcing the Lord's death until he comes again" (1 COR. 11:25-26).

✓ ⸻ LIVING IN ALIGNMENT WITH THE WORD OF GOD ⸻

☐ Do I regularly take communion?
☐ Do I examine myself before I take communion?
☐ Do I use the word of God to determine what is true or another source?
☐ Am I teaching others the truths of the word of God?
☐ In what way is Christ revealing Himself to me?
☐ Do I speak words of life? Does it matter if I curse?

FAITH IN ACTION: TAKE COMMUNION

• Take communion at your church or perhaps you can initiate serving communion at your home with your family. Get creative on when and where you might share communion.

More ideas at GreatWithGod.com

Appeal to Heaven: Use the **High Priestly Blessings Index** to acknowledge Jesus Christ as the **Word of God.**

Wisbit Tip: Speak blessings from Deut. 28 and Isa. 58.

Sunday: May the Lord Bless You. "If you fully obey the Lord your God and carefully keep all His commands that I am giving you today, the Lord Your God will set you high above all the nations of the world."

Monday: May the Lord Keep You. "…Then your light will shine out from the darkness, and the darkness around you will be as bright as noon. The Lord will guide you continually…and restore Your strength…."

Tuesday: May the Lord Smile Upon You. "The Lord will conquer your enemies when they attack you. They will attack you from one direction, but they will scatter from you in seven!"

Wednesday: May the Lord Be Gracious to You. "If you obey the commands of the Lord your God and walk in His ways, the Lord will bless everything you do and will bless you in the land He is giving you."

Thursday: May the Lord Show You His Favor. "The Lord will give you prosperity in the land He swore to your ancestors to give you."

Friday: May the Lord Give You His Peace. "The Lord will bless all the work you do. You will lend to many nations, but you will never need to borrow from them."

Saturday: Blessed to be a Blessing. "May the Lord make you the head and not the tail. Then all the nations of the world will see that you belong to the Lord."

Servant

THE IMAGE OF GOD: "Let this mind be in you which was also in Christ Jesus, who, being in the form of God, did not consider it robbery to be equal with God, but made Himself of no reputation, taking the form of a bond servant, and coming in the likeness of men. And being found in appearance as a man, He humbled Himself and became obedient to the point of death, even the death of the cross. Therefore, God also has highly exalted Him and given Him the name which is above every name" (PHIL. 2:5-9).

▪ "Look at My servant, whom I strengthen. He is My Chosen One, who pleases Me. I have put My Spirit upon Him. He will bring justice to the nations" (Is. 42:1).

— BE A SERVANT —

THE COMMAND OF CHRIST: "But among you it will be different. Whoever wants to be a leader among you must be your servant, and whoever wants to be first among you must become your slave. For even the Son of Man came not to be served but to serve others and to give his life as a ransom for many" (MATT. 20:26-28).

▪ "Work willingly at whatever you do, as though you were working for the Lord rather than for people. Remember that the Lord will give you an inheritance as your reward, and that the Master you are serving is Christ" (COL. 3:23-24).

▪ "And if you give even a cup of cold water to one of the least of my followers, you will surely be rewarded" (MATT. 10:42).

- "The greatest among you must be a servant. But those who exalt themselves will be humbled, and those who humble themselves will be exalted" (MATT. 23:11-12).

- "Therefore humble yourselves under the mighty hand of God, that He may exalt you in due time" (1 PET. 5:6).

- "He sat down, called the twelve disciples over to him, and said, 'Whoever wants to be first must take last place and be the servant of everyone else'" (MARK 9:35).

✓
— LIVING IN ALIGNMENT WITH JESUS THE SERVANT —

☐ How did Jesus demonstrate that He came to serve?

☐ How can Jesus be both servant and King?

☐ What does it mean to be a servant leader?

☐ What are the distinctive attitudes of a servant?

☐ What would it look like in my life to become the servant to servants?

☐ Have I died to all my selfish ambitions?

☐ Do I arrange my schedule to accommodate the wishes of those God has called me to serve?

☐ Do I serve as unto the Lord or for the praise of men?

FAITH IN ACTION: AT-HOME KINDNESS INITIATIVE

- Do a practical task or chore around your house. The key is doing something before being asked and something you usually do not do. Do it with excellence as unto the Lord. No thanks is needed.

- Cook ▪ Wash the dishes ▪ Mow the yard

- Wash and vacuum the car ▪ Do laundry

More ideas at GreatWithGod.com

Appeal to Heaven: Use the **High Priestly Blessings Index** to acknowledge that Jesus Christ came as a servant.

Sunday: May the Lord Bless You. Lord, how shall I seek a blessing for myself, when You set the example of a life of service to others? Lord, help me to serve others that I might be Your source of blessing to them.

Monday: May the Lord Keep You. You, O Lord, are always vigilant. You can protect from storms or You can protect me while I am in the midst of storms. Lord, keep me today. My hope is in You alone.

Tuesday: May the Lord Smile Upon You. Lord, I want to be great for You. I want You to have good reason to smile upon me. Show me today, Lord, whom I might serve. Give me creativity to be a productive servant.

Wednesday: May the Lord Be Gracious to You. Lord, give me Your power to serve beyond my natural strength.

Thursday: May the Lord Show You His Favor. Lord, show me Your mercy as I show mercy to others.

Friday: May the Lord Give You His Peace. The servant of the Lord is not to be filled with selfish ambition. Lord, forgive me for pursuing my own agenda. Today I stop fighting against You. I surrender to You. I ask that Your kingdom come and Your will be done in my life. Fill me with Your peace.

Saturday: Blessed to be a Blessing. The Lord of Angel armies, give me the heart of a servant. It is my prayer and ambition that I might be a servant like You. Serve through me.

18 *the Sacrificial Lamb*

THE IMAGE OF GOD: "The next day John saw Jesus coming toward him and said, 'Look! The Lamb of God who takes away the sin of the world!'" (JN. 1:29)

- "Get rid of the old 'yeast' by removing this wicked person from among you. Then you will be like a fresh batch of dough made without yeast, which is what you really are. Christ, our Passover Lamb, has been sacrificed for us" (1 COR. 5:7).
- "And they sang in a mighty chorus: 'Worthy is the Lamb who was slaughtered—to receive power and riches and wisdom and strength and honor and glory and blessing'"(REV. 5:12).

— BE PERFECT —

THE COMMAND OF CHRIST: "If you love only those who love you, what reward is there for that? Even corrupt tax collectors do that much. If you are kind only to your friends, how are you different from anyone else? Even pagans do that. But you are to be perfect, even as your Father in heaven is perfect" (MATT. 5:46-48).

- "For the eyes of the Lord run to and fro throughout the whole earth, to shew himself strong in the behalf of them whose heart is perfect toward him. Herein thou hast done foolishly: therefore from henceforth thou shalt have wars" (2 CHRON. 16:9 KJV).
- "So we tell others about Christ, warning everyone and teaching everyone with all the wisdom God has given us. We want to present them to God, perfect in their relationship to Christ" (COL. 1:28).

GOD'S PROMISES: TO HONOR THE SACRIFICE OF HIS SON, THE PERFECT LAMB

- "And then I heard every creature in heaven and on earth and under the earth and in the sea. They sang: 'Blessing and honor and glory and power belong to the one sitting on the throne and to the Lamb forever and ever'" (REV. 5:13).
- "For you know that God paid a ransom to save you from the empty life you inherited from your ancestors. And it was not paid with mere gold or silver, which lose their value. It was the precious blood of Christ, the sinless, spotless Lamb of God. God chose him as your ransom long before the world began, but now in these last days he has been revealed for your sake" (1 PET. 1:18-20).

✓ –– LIVING IN ALIGNMENT WITH THE LAMB OF GOD ––

☐ What does it mean that Jesus is my sacrificial lamb?
☐ How can I demonstrate my gratefulness to Jesus for the sacrifice He made on the cross on my behalf?
☐ How can I demonstrate the love of God to people from other cultures?
☐ What does Jesus mean when He says, "Be perfect, even as your Father in heaven is perfect?"
☐ How do I know if I am maturing?

FAITH IN ACTION: A 36-HOUR FAST

- Choose a day this week to pray and fast. No food until breakfast the following day. Drink only water. Slow down and seek God, don't just fast and work harder. Replace your meal times with scripture reading, prayer and volunteering. Fast for a breakthrough. Answer the question, "Why am I fasting?" Read Isaiah 58.

More ideas at GreatWithGod.com

Appeal to Heaven: Use the **High Priestly Blessings Index** to acknowledge Jesus as our sacrificial lamb.

Sunday: May the Lord Bless You. Lord, You loved me so much that You gave Your life as a sacrificial substitute that I might be blessed with eternal life. Lord, I praise You for this inestimable blessing.

Monday: May the Lord Keep You. God, You are for me, so who can stand against me? Keep me today and deliver me from evil.

Tuesday: May the Lord Smile Upon You. Lord, I know that I am unworthy, but You have imputed to me Your righteousness. I am positioned before God as Your fellow heir.

Wednesday: May the Lord Be Gracious to You. Lord God, give me the power to live in the fullness of the Holy Spirit. Bless me with the both the will and to power to do Your good pleasure.

Thursday: May the Lord Show You His Favor. Lord, You are without partiality. Thank You for loving me when I feel unlovable. Cause me to be a channel of Your love to all people.

Friday: May the Lord Give You His Peace. Father, You desire me to live in peace as much as it is up to me. Increase my faith so I can enjoy Your peace.

Saturday: Blessed to be a Blessing. My prayer is simply to present my body to You as a living sacrifice. Make me a vessel of peace.

19 *Lord Jesus Christ*
MESSIAH

THE IMAGE OF GOD: "Then he asked them, 'But who do you say I am?' Simon Peter answered, 'You are the Messiah, the Son of the living God'" (MATT. 16:15-16).

- "Though he was God, he did not think of equality with God as something to cling to. Instead, he gave up his divine privileges; he took the humble position of a slave and was born as a human being. When he appeared in human form, he humbled himself in obedience to God and died a criminal's death on a cross. Therefore, God elevated him to the place of highest honor and gave him the name above all other names, that at the name of Jesus every knee should bow, in heaven and on earth and under the earth, and every tongue declare that Jesus Christ is Lord, to the glory of God the Father" (PHIL. 2:6-11).

- "...you are to name him Jesus, for he will save his people from their sins" (MATT. 1:21).

— BE RECONCILED —

THE COMMAND OF CHRIST: "So if you are presenting a sacrifice at the altar in the Temple and you suddenly remember that someone has something against you, leave your sacrifice there at the altar. Go and be reconciled to that person. Then come and offer your sacrifice to God" (MATT. 5:23-24).

- "For God was in Christ, reconciling the world to himself, no longer counting people's sins against them. And he gave us this wonderful message of reconciliation. So we are Christ's ambassadors; God is making his appeal through us. We speak for Christ when we plead, 'Come back to God!'" (2 COR. 5:19-20).

- "But Christ has rescued us from the curse pronounced by the law. When he was hung on the cross, he took upon himself the curse for our wrongdoing. For it is written in the Scriptures, 'Cursed is everyone who is hung on a tree.' Through Christ Jesus, God has blessed the Gentiles with the same blessing he promised to Abraham, so that we who are believers might receive the promised Holy Spirit through faith" (GAL. 3:13-14).

- "Giving thanks to the Father who has qualified us to be partakers of the inheritance of the saints in the light. He has delivered us from the power of darkness and conveyed us into the kingdom of the Son of His love" (COL. 1:12-13).

✓   —— LIVING IN ALIGNMENT WITH JESUS AS LORD ——

☐   What does it mean that Jesus is Lord?

☐   What does it mean that Jesus is Christ?

☐   How can I demonstrate my gratefulness to God for coming to deliver me from powers of darkness and sin?

☐   What is does it mean to be redeemed from under the curse of the law?

☐   Have I sought reconciliation from those I have offended?

☐   What does it mean to have a clear conscience?

FAITH IN ACTION: MEND BROKEN RELATIONSHIPS

- Do you have an unresolved grievance? Seek reconciliation and forgiveness from those whom the Holy Spirit has convicted you that you have wronged. Forgive those who have wronged you.

More ideas at GreatWithGod.com

Appeal to Heaven: Use the **High Priestly Blessings Index** to acknowledge the lordship of Jesus Christ.

Sunday: May the Lord Bless You. Lord Jesus, You came as Messiah to offer deliverance from sin and the blessing of eternal life to all who accept You. I accept You and thank You that my name is written in the book of life.

Monday: May the Lord Keep You. There is no other who can keep and protect like the Lord God almighty. That which is Yours You are able to keep. Lord, keep my family this day.

Tuesday: May the Lord Smile Upon You. Lord Jesus, while we were yet sinners You came and died for us. Your compassion was manifested in kindness. I ask You to remember I am but dust. Be kind to my family in every way.

Wednesday: May the Lord Be Gracious to You. Messiah, You came that we might have life and life more abundantly. Give my family this day the power and desire to live a victorious Christian life.

Thursday: May the Lord Show You His Favor. Jesus Messiah, You came into the world and proclaimed the favorable year of the Lord. Today redeem my family from the bondage of sin.

Friday: May the Lord Give You His Peace. Lord, help me make peace with those I have offended. Today is the day of reconciliation.

Saturday: Blessed to be a Blessing. Praise be to the Father, the Son and the Holy Spirit. You are the mysterious three in one. My prayer is simply to present my body to You, the triune God, as a living sacrifice this day. Make me an ambassador of reconciliation.

King

THE IMAGE OF GOD: "On his robe at his thigh was written this title: 'King of all kings and Lord of all lords'" (MARK 15:26).

- "A sign announced the charge against him. It read, 'The King of the Jews'"(Is. 9:6).
- "Yours, O LORD, is the greatness, the power, the glory, the victory, and the majesty. Everything in the heavens and on earth is yours, O LORD, and this is your kingdom. We adore you as the one who is over all things. Wealth and honor come from you alone, for you rule over everything. Power and might are in your hand, and at your discretion people are made great and given strength" (1 CHRON. 29:11-12).

— RENDER TO CAESAR —

THE COMMAND OF CHRIST: "'Here, show me the coin used for the tax.' When they handed him a Roman coin, he asked, 'Whose picture and title are stamped on it?' 'Caesar's,' they replied. 'Well, then,' he said, 'give to Caesar what belongs to Caesar, and give to God what belongs to God'" (MATT. 22:19-21).

- "Respect everyone, and love the family of believers. Fear God, and respect the king" (1 PET. 2:17).
- "For the Lord's sake, submit to all human authority—whether the king as head of state, or the officials he has appointed. For the king has sent them to punish those who do wrong and to honor those who do right" (1 PET. 2:13-14).

▪ "Therefore, God elevated him to the place of highest honor and gave him the name above all other names, that at the name of Jesus every knee should bow, in heaven and on earth and under the earth, and every tongue declare that Jesus Christ is Lord, to the glory of God the Father" (PHIL. 2:9-11).

▪ "Jesus answered, 'My Kingdom is not an earthly kingdom. If it were, my followers would fight to keep me from being handed over to the Jewish leaders. But my Kingdom is not of this world.' Pilate said, 'So you are a king?' Jesus responded, 'You say I am a king. Actually, I was born and came into the world to testify to the truth. All who love the truth recognize that what I say is true'" (JN. 18:36-37).

▪ "Pray this way for kings and all who are in authority so that we can live peaceful and quiet lives marked by godliness and dignity" (1 TIM. 2:2).

✓   ⸺ LIVING IN ALIGNMENT WITH GOD AS KING ⸺

☐ What makes a king a king?

☐ What does it mean that Jesus reigns?

☐ If Jesus is King why does He command that I submit to all human authority?

☐ How can I honor my authorities?

FAITH IN ACTION: CITY JERICHO PRAYER WALK

▪ Do a Jericho prayer walk at your city hall or another strategic location. Pray: 1) For God's kingdom to come to your community/city. 2) For Christ to deliver your city from powers of darkness. 3) For God to comfort those who are oppressed. 4) Remove sources of temptation. 5) To raise up and to send disciple making laborers to your city.

More ideas at GreatWithGod.com

APPEAL TO HEAVEN: Use the **High Priestly Blessings Index** to acknowledge that Jesus Christ is our King.

SUNDAY: MAY THE LORD BLESS YOU. Lord, You have redeemed me from the curse of the law, having been made a curse for me, for it is written cursed is everyone that hangs upon on a tree. Let the blessing of Abraham come upon me.

MONDAY: MAY THE LORD KEEP YOU. Whom shall I fear? God is for me; who can stand against me? Lord, protect me and grant that my heart will be made courageous.

TUESDAY: MAY THE LORD SMILE UPON YOU. God, smile upon me and let the grace of our Lord Jesus Christ, who was rich but became poor for our sake, be upon me.

WEDNESDAY: MAY THE LORD BE GRACIOUS TO YOU. Lord, You oppose the proud but give grace to the humble. I kneel now before my King. I admit that I am nothing without You. Bless me with power to obey Your commands.

THURSDAY: MAY THE LORD SHOW YOU HIS FAVOR. I ask of You to give me life abundant and help me to manifest it to others that they may also partake of abundant life.

FRIDAY: MAY THE LORD GIVE YOU HIS PEACE. King Jesus, You are indeed the Prince of Peace. Lord, I pray now, let there be peace in Jerusalem, for You have commanded me to do so.

SATURDAY: BLESSED TO BE A BLESSING. You came the first time to earth as the Lamb to deliver us from bondage to sin. And then You went to heaven to prepare a place for me. Now, I pray for Your quick return, for I know that this second coming reveals You as King of kings. Even so, come and rule.

High Priest

THE IMAGE OF GOD: "So then, since we have a great High Priest who has entered heaven, Jesus the Son of God, let us hold firmly to what we believe. This High Priest of ours understands our weaknesses, for he faced all of the same testings we do, yet he did not sin. So let us come boldly to the throne of our gracious God. There we will receive his mercy, and we will find grace to help us when we need it most" (HEB. 4:14-16).

▪ "Jesus became a priest, not by meeting the physical requirement of belonging to the tribe of Levi, but by the power of a life that cannot be destroyed. And the psalmist pointed this out when he prophesied, 'You are a priest forever in the order of Melchizedek'" (HEB. 7:16-17).

— PRAY FOR LABORERS —

THE COMMAND OF CHRIST: "He said to his disciples, 'The harvest is great, but the workers are few. So pray to the Lord who is in charge of the harvest; ask him to send more workers into his fields'" (MATT. 9:37-38).

▪ "But how can they call on him to save them unless they believe in him? And how can they believe in him if they have never heard about him? And how can they hear about him unless someone tells them? And how will anyone go and tell them without being sent?" (ROM. 10:14).

▪ "I looked for someone who might rebuild the wall of righteousness that guards the land. I searched for someone to stand in the gap in the wall so I wouldn't have to destroy the land, but I found no one. So now I will pour out my fury on them, consuming them with the fire of my anger" (EZE. 22:30-31).

GOD'S PROMISES: FOR CHRIST TO MEDIATE
A BLESSING INSTEAD OF A CURSE

- "And you are living stones that God is building into His spiritual temple. What's more, you are His Holy Priests. Through the mediation of Jesus Christ, you offer spiritual sacrifices that please God" (1 PET. 2:5).
- "Your towns and your fields will be blessed. Your children and your crops will be blessed. The offspring of your herds and flocks will be blessed. Your fruit baskets and breadboards will be blessed. Wherever you go and whatever you do, you will be blessed" (DEUT. 28:1-6).

✓ —— LIVING IN ALIGNMENT WITH JESUS MY HIGH PRIEST ——

- ☐ What does it mean to have Jesus as my high priest? What is the role of a priest?
- ☐ How could understanding Jesus as high priest impact my prayer life?
- ☐ What does it mean for God's people to be a kingdom of priests? Does that make me a priest?
- ☐ What does it mean to stand in the gap and pray?
- ☐ What fields can I identify that need more laborers?

FAITH IN ACTION: PRAY FOR LABORERS

- Pray that the Holy Spirit would raise up laborers to go to the ends of the earth for God's kingdom that salvation may come to every nation, tribe, people and language. Put your hand on a map or globe and pray for God to raise up and send missionaries to a specific country. Ask God to send disciple makers to a specific ethnic group.

More ideas at GreatWithGod.com

APPEAL TO HEAVEN: Use the **High Priestly Blessings Index** to acknowledge that Jesus is our High Priest.

SUNDAY: MAY THE LORD BLESS YOU. Lord Jesus, You are the one true high priest; whomsoever You bless will indeed be blessed. I ask You to bless me this day as You did the children who came to You. Make me the head and not the tail.

MONDAY: MAY THE LORD KEEP YOU. Lord God, I thank You that You are my protector, and as my high priest I have an advocate who pleads for me before God as my atonement and defends me from my accusers.

TUESDAY: MAY THE LORD SMILE UPON YOU. God, be kind to me today. Please be gentle and patient with my slowness to respond to You.

WEDNESDAY: MAY THE LORD BE GRACIOUS TO YOU. Lord, I need Your grace; give me this day my daily portion of power that I might fulfill all the good works You have for me.

THURSDAY: MAY THE LORD SHOW YOU HIS FAVOR. Lord, the difference between failure and success is Your favor. Please grant me Your unfailing favor today that I might bring glory to Your name.

FRIDAY: MAY THE LORD GIVE YOU HIS PEACE. Lord, I thank You that You said You give peace, not as the world gives but as God gives. Lord, I need Your peace. Comfort my fearful heart.

SATURDAY: BLESSED TO BE A BLESSING. Hear, O Israel. The Lord our God is one Lord: (DEUT. 6:4). Lord, it is the desire of my heart that I might know You and the power of Your resurrection and fellowship of Your sufferings. Here I am; send me as a laborer into Your harvest.

$\mathcal{I}$ AM THE MESSIAH

THE "I AM" SAYINGS OF CHRIST

PRAY USING "R" YOU PRAYING INDEX WHEEL

YOUR GOAL: PRAY THROUGH THE "R" YOU
PRAYING INDEX EACH DAY. AND THEN PRAY FOR
FIVE MINUTES CONCERNING THE INDEX THEME
ASSIGNED FOR EACH DAY. USE THE PRAYER GUIDE
AT THE END OF EACH CHAPTER
TO HELP GET STARTED.

ON SATURDAY, COMPLETE YOUR MEDITATION FOR
THE WEEK BY PRAYING COMPLETELY THROUGH THE
PRAYER WHEEL INDEX IN 35 MINUTES.

WISBIT TIP: MAKE A PROMISE TO GOD TO BE
AVAILABLE TO RENDER HELP TO OBVIOUS SERVICE
OPPORTUNITIES THAT COME ACROSS YOUR PATH
FOR THE NEXT 6 WEEKS.

"R" YOU PRAYING INDEX WHEEL

Lord God Almighty, I pause to **Reflect** on the awesome fact that You are God who created everything. I am amazed You are interested in me but my spirit bears witness within me that You are indeed my loving Father. I admit, I have played the part of the prodigal son. I **Repent**; forgive me and take me back. Your love never ceases, and I **Rejoice** that Your mercies are new every morning. Jesus, **Rebuke** Satan away from me that I might not sin against You. Instead, I ask the Holy Spirit to **Release** ministries, let there be laborers to feed Your disciples. I **Recommit** myself; here I am; send me. Speak to me now for I am ready to **Receive**. Amen.

"R" You Praying Index Wheel

22 —the *Light of the World*

THE IMAGE OF GOD: "Jesus spoke to the people once more and said, 'I am the light of the world. If you follow Me, you won't have to walk in darkness, because you will have the light that leads to life'" (JN. 8:12).

▪ "The Word gave life to everything that was created, and His life brought light to everyone. The light shines in the darkness, and the darkness can never extinguish it" (JN. 1:1-5).

▪ "This is the message we heard from Jesus and now declare to you: God is light, and there is no darkness in him at all. ...But if we are living in the light, as God is in the light, then we have fellowship with each other, and the blood of Jesus, his Son, cleanses us from all sin" (1 JN. 1:5-7).

— LET YOUR LIGHT SHINE —

THE COMMAND OF CHRIST: "You are the light of the world—like a city on a hilltop that cannot be hidden. No one lights a lamp and then puts it under a basket. Instead, a lamp is placed on a stand, where it gives light to everyone in the house. In the same way, let your good deeds shine out for all to see, so that everyone will praise your heavenly Father" (MATT. 5:14-16).

▪ "Then the King will say to those on his right, 'Come, you who are blessed by my Father, inherit the Kingdom prepared for you from the creation of the world. For I was hungry, and you fed me. I was thirsty, and you gave me a drink. I was a stranger, and you invited me into your home. I was naked, and you gave me clothing. I was sick, and you cared for me. I was in prison, and you visited me'" (MATT. 25:34-36).

- "When Moses came down from Mount Sinai carrying the two stone tablets inscribed with the terms of the covenant, he wasn't aware that his face had become radiant because he had spoken to the LORD" (Ex. 34:29).
- "If anyone claims, 'I am living in the light,' but hates a fellow believer, that person is still living in darkness. Anyone who loves a fellow believer is living in the light and does not cause others to stumble" (1 JN. 2:9-10).

✓ — **LIVING IN ALIGNMENT WITH THE LIGHT OF THE WORLD** —

☐ Do I daily spend time in God's presence so I can be a reflection of His glory?

☐ Have I stopped participating in those things that are spiritual darkness?

☐ Do I daily look for ways to be doing good works?

☐ Am I active in bringing the light of Christ to the nations of the world?

☐ Do I bring myself to the light to let God examine me to see if there be any wicked way in me?

☐ What does it mean that Jesus is the Light of the world?

☐ What does it mean that I am the light of the world?

☐ On a scale of 1-10 how available am I to offer practical help to others in need?

FAITH IN ACTION: LAUNCH A LANTERN

- Launch a sky lantern this week or launch a water lantern into a pond, lake, or river. Do this with another person or a small group of people to honor someone who is effectively sharing the love of Christ.

More ideas at GreatWithGod.com

APPEAL TO HEAVEN: Use the "R" You Praying Index to acknowledge that Jesus is the Light of the World.

SUNDAY: REFLECT. Lord Jesus, You are indeed the light of the world. Light is a symbol of Your holiness and insight. I am unable to hide from You and I cannot be lost where You cannot find me.

MONDAY: REPENT. Lord, Your light is like a candle which exposes my hidden motives. I find them now tainted with selfish ambition, greed and pride. Lord, forgive me and change me from the inside out.

TUESDAY: REJOICE. I rejoice in Your light. I have all the insight I need in You alone. Your light is my salvation. You are my guiding light. All thanks to You I have purpose with which to live. I want to live in the light.

WEDNESDAY: RESIST. Lord Jesus, I ask You now to bind and rebuke the powers of darkness today from my family, my church, my school, my place of work.

THURSDAY: RELEASE. Lord Jesus, raise up laborers to go forth as ambassadors of Your light. Release teaching ministries that will raise up Your standard of truth in my church.

FRIDAY: RECOMMIT. Lord Jesus, You said I am the light of the whole world. God, I recommit today to make sure my outreach, my giving and praying extend far beyond my city and state, for You are the Light of the whole world.

SATURDAY: RECEIVE. Lord, what did You mean when You said, "I am the light of the World?" I will quiet myself to listen to You speak.

23

the Bread of Life

THE IMAGE OF GOD: "Jesus said, 'I tell you the truth, Moses didn't give you bread from heaven. My Father did. And now He offers you the true bread f rom heaven. The true bread of God is the one who comes down f rom heaven and gives life to the world.'" 'Sir,' they said, 'give us that bread every day.' Jesus replied, 'I am the bread of life. Whoever comes to Me will never be hungry again. Whoever believes in Me will never be thirsty'" (JN. 6:32-35).

▪ "Anyone who eats the bread from heaven, however, will never die. I am the living bread that came down from heaven. Anyone who eats this bread will live forever; and this bread, which I will offer so the world may live, is my flesh" (JN. 6:50-51).

— FEED ON GOD'S WORD —

THE COMMAND OF CHRIST: "But Jesus told him, 'No! The Scriptures say, 'People do not live by bread alone, but by every word that comes from the mouth of God'"(MATT. 4:4).

▪ "Study this Book of Instruction continually. Meditate on it day and night so you will be sure to obey everything written in it. Only then will you prosper and succeed in all you do" (JOSH. 1:8).

▪ "And you must commit yourselves wholeheartedly to these commands that I am giving you today. Repeat them again and again to your children. Talk about them when you are at home and when you are on the road, when you are going to bed and when you are getting up" (DEUT. 6:6-7).

- "He that hath my commandments and keeps them…and (I) will manifest myself to him" (Jn. 14:21).
- "For the word of God is alive and powerful. It is sharper than the sharpest two-edged sword, cutting between soul and spirit, between joint and marrow. It exposes our inner-most thoughts and desires" (Heb. 4:12).
- "All Scripture is inspired by God and is useful to teach us what is true and to make us realize what is wrong in our lives. It corrects us when we are wrong and teaches us to do what is right" (2 Tim. 3:16).
- "Thy word have I hid in my heart that I might not sin against thee" (Ps. 119:11 kjv).
- "So faith comes from hearing, that is, hearing the Good News about Christ" (Rom. 10:17).

✓ —— LIVING IN ALIGNMENT WITH THE BREAD OF LIFE ——
- ☐ Am I reading the word of God daily?
- ☐ Am I available to offer practical help to those in need?
- ☐ How can I increase my spiritual diet?
- ☐ Do I ask God to search my desires, my will, and emotions to see if there is any wicked way in me?
- ☐ What is the relationship between faith and God's word?
- ☐ Am I memorizing and meditating on the words of Christ?

FAITH IN ACTION: SWEET BREAD

- "For I was hungry, and you fed Me."
- Bless those attending some gathering this week by delivering donuts, cookies, or cake. If they ask why, say, "I wanted to share the love of God in a practical way; no strings attached. Enjoy!"

More ideas at GreatWithGod.com

Appeal to Heaven: Use the "R" You Praying Index to acknowledge that Jesus is the Bread of Life.

Wisbit Tip: Pray outdoors, pray as You walk, or find (create) a sacred place outside where You can go and pray.

Sunday: Reflect. It is true that I do not live by bread alone but by every word that proceeds from Your mouth. I am primarily a spirit. Please teach me how to grow to be mighty in spirit.

Monday: Repent. Lord, give me a repentant heart. Search me and see if there be any wicked way in me.

Tuesday: Rejoice. I give thanks for Your goodness and provision. I recognize every good gift, even my daily bread, comes from You.

Wednesday: Resist. Lord, enable me to stand against the powers of darkness; defend me, protect me, deliver me and come be my shield.

Thursday: Release. God, raise up ministries and ministers that as of yet do not exist. Share Your dreams with me. Let my heart dream Your dreams.

Friday: Re-Commit. I fully surrender to Christ. Help me fulfill my role in Your unchanging purpose for the world.

Saturday: Receive. Lord, give me today my daily bread. I am ready to listen. What is my next step concerning_____? (Quietly listen to the still small voice within You). Perhaps write down His answer.

the True Vine

THE IMAGE OF GOD: "I am the true grapevine, and my Father is the Gardener. He cuts off every branch of mine that doesn't produce fruit, and He prunes the branches that do bear fruit so they will produce even more" (JN. 15:1-2).

- "Yes, I am the vine; you are the branches. Those who remain in Me, and I in them, will produce much fruit. For apart from Me you can do nothing. Anyone who does not remain in Me is thrown away like a useless branch and withers. Such branches are gathered into a pile to be burned. But if you remain in Me and My words remain in you, you may ask for anything you want, and it will be granted! When you produce much fruit, you are My true disciples. This brings great glory to My Father" (JN. 15:5-8).

— DESPISE NOT LITTLE ONES —

THE COMMAND OF CHRIST: "Beware that you don't look down on any of these little ones. For I tell you that in heaven their angels are always in the presence of my heavenly Father" (MATT. 18:10).

- "Then he said, 'I tell you the truth, unless you turn from your sins and become like little children, you will never get into the Kingdom of Heaven. So anyone who becomes as humble as this little child is the greatest in the Kingdom of Heaven'" (MATT. 18:3-4).

- "But Jesus said, 'Let the children come to me. Don't stop them! For the Kingdom of Heaven belongs to those who are like these children'" (MATT 19:14).

▪ "For if the roots of the tree are holy, the branches will be, too. But some of these branches from Abraham's tree—some of the people of Israel—have been broken off. And you Gentiles, who were branches from a wild olive tree, have been grafted in. So now you also receive the blessing God has promised Abraham and his children, sharing in the rich nourishment from the root of God's special olive tree" (ROM. 11:16-18).

▪ "Beware of false prophets who come disguised as harmless sheep but are really vicious wolves. You can identify them by their fruit, that is, by the way they act" (MATT. 7:15-16).

▪ "Wherefore lay apart all filthiness and superfluity of naughtiness, and receive with meekness the engrafted word, which is able to save your souls" (JAM. 1:21 KJV).

✓   — LIVING IN ALIGNMENT WITH THE TRUE VINE —

☐ How can I maintain a living communion with Jesus?
☐ Do I regularly take time to engraft God's word into my heart through memorization and meditation?
☐ Do I respond to others with patience, kindness?
☐ Is there evidence of gentleness and self-control in me?
☐ Do I investigate the fruit of those who wish to teach me?

FAITH IN ACTION: GIVE A DRINK

▪ "I was thirsty, and you gave Me a drink."
▪ Buy a single drink or a case of water bottles and deliver them to someone or some group intentionally. If they ask why, you might say, "I'm just sharing the love and trying to pay it forward."

More ideas at GreatWithGod.com

APPEAL TO HEAVEN: Use the **"R" You Praying Index** to acknowledge Jesus as the True Vine.

SUNDAY: REFLECT. You are the vine and I am a branch. You are my source of life. My prayer is to stay connected to You and to help others become connected to You. Teach me daily how to abide in Your presence.

MONDAY: REPENT. Too often, Lord, I go rogue, thinking I can do life without You. I cannot. I am reminded today that You made me to depend on You for everything. Lord, today I turn from the world to cling to You.

TUESDAY: REJOICE. I rejoice for You have grafted me, a wild branch, into Your family. All my provision and protection comes from resting in Your redemption. I stop and recognize right now that the good things I have in my life are from You. Thank You.

WEDNESDAY: RESIST. Father, teach me to discern the false prophets which come to me disguised in sheep's clothing. Help me see the good deeds done with right attitudes. And make me able to discern the deceit of false teachers.

THURSDAY: RELEASE. Lord Jesus, let there be a release of ministries of reconciliation launched in the local churches in my city. Raise up ministries to teach disciples how to abide in You and intercede for the lost.

FRIDAY: RECOMMIT. Lord, here I am. Send me. I want to be Your ambassador of reconciliation. Give me boldness to preach Your message, "Come back to God!"

SATURDAY: RECEIVE. Lord, what is my destiny? What type of fruit do You want my life to bring forth?

—the Gate

THE IMAGE OF GOD: "So he explained it to them: 'I tell you the truth, I am the gate for the sheep. All who came before me were thieves and robbers. But the true sheep did not listen to them. Yes, I am the gate. Those who come in through me will be saved. They will come and go freely and will find good pastures'" (JN. 10:7-9).

▪ "There is salvation in no one else! God has given no other name under heaven by which we must be saved" (ACTS 4:12).

—— MAKE DISCIPLES ——

THE COMMAND OF CHRIST: "Therefore, go and make disciples of all the nations, baptizing them in the name of the Father and the Son and the Holy Spirit. Teach these new disciples to obey all the commands I have given you. And be sure of this: I am with you always, even to the end of the age" (MATT. 28:19-20).

▪ "You have heard me teach things that have been confirmed by many reliable witnesses. Now teach these truths to other trustworthy people who will be able to pass them on to others" (2 TIM. 2:2).

▪ "The Spirit of the Lord is upon me, for he has anointed me to bring Good News to the poor. He has sent me to proclaim that captives will be released, that the blind will see, that the oppressed will be set free, and that the time of the Lord's favor has come" (LUKE 4:18 -19).

▪ "But you will receive power when the Holy Spirit comes upon you. And you will be my witnesses, telling people about me everywhere—in Jerusalem, throughout Judea, in Samaria, and to the ends of the earth" (ACTS 1:8).

GOD'S PROMISES: TO USE HIS DISCIPLES TO GRANT SALVATION THROUGH JESUS CHRIST

- "Then Paul said, 'John indeed baptized with a baptism of repentance, saying to the people that they should believe on Him who would come after Him, that is, on Christ Jesus.' When they heard this, they were baptized in the name of the Lord Jesus" (ACTS 19:4-6).
- "You can enter God's Kingdom only through the narrow gate. The highway to hell is broad, and its gate is wide for the many who choose that way. But the gateway to life is very narrow and the road is difficult, and only a few ever find it" (MATT. 7:13).

— LIVING IN ALIGNMENT WITH THE GATE —

✓

- ☐ Have I rejected the easy paths of false doors of opportunity offering short cut access to authentic spirituality?
- ☐ Am I making disciples of Jesus Christ?
- ☐ Am I studying the commands of Christ so I can teach them to others?
- ☐ Am I convinced that there is no other gate to eternal life except through Christ alone?
- ☐ Am I striving to follow the narrow path of discipleship by regularly practicing daily disciplines?
- ☐ Do I share the gospel with those beyond my ethnicity?

FAITH IN ACTION: WELCOME STRANGERS

- "I was a stranger, and you invited Me into your home."
- Find a way to open the welcome door of brotherhood. Look for the new person, look for the outsider. Go out of your way to shake hands, say hello, and ask their name. Sit with them or near them if it's a group gathering.

More ideas at GreatWithGod.com

Appeal to Heaven: Use the "R" You Praying Index to acknowledge that Jesus is the Gate.

Sunday: Reflect. Jesus, since it is true that there is no other name given among men by which we must be saved, give me courage and creativity to share this urgent truth with others.

Monday: Repent. Lord, I believe and yet help my unbelief. Too often, Lord, I live in such a way that betrays what I know to be truth. Have mercy on me lord, forgive me and give me power to change.

Tuesday: Rejoice. Lord, I give thanks and I rejoice that my name is written in the Lamb's Book of Life. My heart rejoices and my spirit bears witness that I am indeed a child of God.

Wednesday: Resist. Lord, You declared after being raised from the dead that all authority in heaven and on earth had been given unto You. I ask You therefore to bind, rebuke and disable every hindering spirit of darkness in my city.

Thursday: Release. Lord let there be evangelistic ministries to children, youth, orphans and widow. Raise up laborers to proclaim the good news. Raise up mentors to make disciples of all nations.

Friday: Recommit. Today, I accept my responsibility to disciple all nations, not just feed, not just clothe, not just house, not just educate, not just offer medical assistance. Help me offer the door of salvation and discipleship to all nations.

Saturday: Receive. Just pause, quiet yourself, and ask God a question. Perhaps you could ask Him, " What part am I to play in making disciples of all nations?" and then listen.

26 *the Resurrection*
AND THE LIFE

THE IMAGE OF GOD: "Jesus told her, 'I am the resurrection and the life. Anyone who believes in Me will live, even after dying. Everyone who lives in Me and believes in Me will never ever die. Do you believe this, Martha?'" (JN. 11:25-26).

▪ "The Father loves Me because I sacrifice My life so I may take it back again. No one can take My life from Me. I sacrifice it voluntarily. For I have the authority to lay it down when I want to and also to take it up again. For this is what My Father has commanded" (JN. 10:17-18).

▪ "Because God's children are human beings—made of flesh and blood—the Son also became flesh and blood. For only as a human being could he die, and only by dying could he break the power of the devil, who had the power of death. Only in this way could he set free all who have lived their lives as slaves to the fear of dying" (HEB. 2:14-15).

— RECEIVE GOD'S POWER —

THE COMMAND OF CHRIST: "But you will receive power when the Holy Spirit comes upon you. And you will be my witnesses, telling people about me everywhere—in Jerusalem, throughout Judea, in Samaria, and to the ends of the earth" (ACTS 1:8).

▪ "For God has not given us a spirit of fear and timidity, but of power, love, and self-discipline" (2 TIM. 1:7).

▪ "And my message and my preaching were very plain. Rather than using clever and persuasive speeches, I relied only on the power of the Holy Spirit" (1 COR. 2:4).

▪ "Again he said, 'Peace be with you. As the Father has sent me, so I am sending you.' Then he breathed on them and said, 'Receive the Holy Spirit'" (Jn. 20:21-22).

▪ "And the Holy Spirit helps us in our weakness. For example, we don't know what God wants us to pray for. But the Holy Spirit prays for us with groanings that cannot be expressed in words. And the Father who knows all hearts knows what the Spirit is saying, for the Spirit pleads for us believers in harmony with God's own will. And we know that God causes everything to work together for the good of those who love God and are called according to his purpose for them" (Rom. 8:26-28).

✓ — LIVING IN ALIGNMENT WITH THE RESURRECTION AND LIFE —

☐ What does the Holy Spirit empower me to be able to do?

☐ How does the Holy Spirit help me pray?

☐ Am I living a life free from the fear of death?

☐ What are the conditions that must be met for me to have faith that all things are working together for my good?

☐ Do I understand that Christ died that I may live?

☐ How can I cultivate the power of the Holy Spirit in my life?

FAITH IN ACTION: GIVE CLOTHES

▪ "I was naked and you clothed Me."

▪ This week go through your closet; identify what you are willing to discard. Deliver to your local ministry center or give to your church for foreign missions.

More ideas at GreatWithGod.com

APPEAL TO HEAVEN: Use the "R" You Praying Index to acknowledge that Jesus is the Resurrection and the Life.

SUNDAY: REFLECT. Lord Jesus, I am comforted by Your sovereignty. You have power over death, for Yourself and all who believe in You. Your resurrection I take as proof that I too will live even after I die.

MONDAY: REPENT. Dear God, I know that the steps to eternal life are that I first confess with my mouth that Jesus is Lord and then believe in my heart that You have raised him from the dead. I believe and I confess You are Lord.

TUESDAY: REJOICE. This is eternal life—to know You, the one true God and Jesus Christ, the one You sent to earth to save us from our sins.

WEDNESDAY: RESIST. Oh God, whom shall I fear? I will not fear those who can take my life but cannot take my soul. You alone have the power to keep my soul beyond the grave. You delivered me from death.

THURSDAY: RELEASE. Let there be a ministry released in my city that will minister in the power of the Holy Spirit. Raise up evangelists and pastors to preach that we must be born again of the Holy Spirit.

FRIDAY: RECOMMIT. Lord, You asked Your disciples to prepare and wait to receive the power of the Holy Spirit. Lord I recommit to You today. Please fill me now with Your Holy Spirit.

SATURDAY: RECEIVE. Lord, what can I do to experience more of Your power in my life? Speak, for I am listening.

27 the Way, the Truth
AND THE LIFE

THE IMAGE OF GOD: "Jesus told him, 'I am the way, the truth, and the life. No one can come to the Father except through me'" (Jn. 14:6).

- "There is salvation in no one else! God has given no other name under heaven by which we must be saved" (Acts 4:12).
- "The thief's purpose is to steal and kill and destroy. My purpose is to give them a rich and satisfying life" (Jn. 10:10).
- "And I will ask the Father, and he will give you another Advocate, who will never leave you. He is the Holy Spirit, who leads into all truth" (Jn. 14:16).

— KEEP MY COMMANDMENTS —

THE COMMAND OF CHRIST: "If you love me, obey my commandments" (Jn. 14:15).

- "He that hath my commandments, and keepeth them, he it is that loveth me: and he that loveth me shall be loved of my Father, and I will love him, and will manifest myself to him" (Jn. 14:21 KJV).
- "And we can be sure that we know him if we obey his commandments. If someone claims, 'I know God,' but doesn't obey God's commandments, that person is a liar and is not living in the truth" (1 Jn. 2:3-4).
- "I have hidden your word in my heart, that I might not sin against you" (Ps. 119:11).
- "But don't just listen to God's word. You must do what it says. Otherwise, you are only fooling yourselves" (Jam. 1:22).

- "Jesus said to the people who believed in Him, 'You are truly My disciples if you remain faithful to My teachings. And you will know the truth, and the truth will set you free'" (JN. 8:31-32).
- "But people who aren't spiritual can't receive these truths from God's Spirit. It all sounds foolish to them and they can't understand it, for only those who are spiritual can understand what the Spirit means" (1 COR. 2:14).
- "But when the Father sends the Advocate as my representative—that is, the Holy Spirit—he will teach you everything and will remind you of everything I have told you" (JN. 14:26).

✓ —— LIVING IN ALIGNMENT WITH THE WAY, TRUTH, AND LIFE ——

☐ What does it mean for Christ to be the truth?
☐ Are the Scriptures the final voice of truth in my life or do I look to other sources for final approval?
☐ Am I pursuing God's truth as the means of my freedom
☐ Do I bring every word of counsel and test it against the veracity of the Scripture?
☐ Do I obey Christ's commands or do I just hear the word?

FAITH IN ACTION: CARE FOR THE ILL

- "I was sick, and you cared for Me."

- Visit and care for someone who is hospitalized/institutionalized/home bound, or in assisted living. This could be a family member. Or volunteer to help the care ministry of your church; but don't go empty-handed: gifts are always appreciated.

More ideas at GreatWithGod.com

APPEAL TO HEAVEN: Use the "R" You Praying Index to acknowledge that Jesus is the Way, the Truth, and the Life.

SUNDAY: REFLECT. One thought dominates my mind today: You shall know the truth and the truth will set You free. Lord, Your very essence is truth. There is no shadow or gray spaces with You, only truth. I want to know You. Make me to know the truth.

MONDAY: REPENT. Lord, I am convicted of my sinfulness for I am full of deception, half-truths, and downright lies. I have misrepresented myself to make myself look good. Have mercy upon me. Your truth convicts me I am altogether undone. Cleanse me from my sin.

TUESDAY: REJOICE. I acknowledged my sin and the Lord forgave me. I rejoice because I have Your truth to guide me to live righteously.

WEDNESDAY: RESIST. Lord Jesus, with Your truth I make my stand against evil. I resist as You modeled for me. Get away from me, Satan: for it is written, thou shalt worship the Lord thy God, and him only shalt thou worship. Amen.

THURSDAY: RELEASE. Lord God, let there be ministries raised up to publish and preach Your truth. Raise up evangelists in my neighborhood. Raise up radio broadcasts around the world to share Your truth in every language on earth.

FRIDAY: RECOMMIT. Lord, I recommit myself to studying the Bible so that I can obey Your commands.

SATURDAY: RECEIVE. Lord, what more can I do to show You that I love You? (Pause) Listen and write the answer You receive from this prayer.

28 *the Good Shepherd*

THE IMAGE OF GOD: "I am the good Shepherd; I know my own sheep, and they know Me, just as My Father knows Me and I know the Father. So, I sacrifice My life for the sheep. I have other sheep, too, that are not in this sheepfold. I must bring them also. They will listen to My voice, and there will be one flock with One Shepherd" (JN. 10:14-16).

▪ "The Lord is my shepherd; I shall not want. He maketh me to lie down in green pastures: he leadeth me beside the still waters. He restoreth my soul: he leadeth me in the paths of righteousness for his name's sake. Yea, though I walk through the valley of the shadow of death, I will fear no evil: for thou art with me; thy rod and thy staff they comfort me" (Ps. 23:1-4 KJV).

▪ "All the nations will be gathered in His presence, and He will separate the people as a shepherd separates the sheep from the goats" (Matt. 25:32).

— FEED MY SHEEP —

THE COMMAND OF CHRIST: "After breakfast Jesus asked Simon, 'Simon, son of John, do you love me more than these?' 'Yes, Lord,' Simon replied, 'you know I love you.' 'Then feed my lambs,' Jesus told him. Jesus repeated the question: 'Peter, son of John, do you love me?' 'Yes, Lord,' Peter said, 'you know I love you.' 'Then take care of my sheep,' Jesus said" (JN. 21:15-16).

▪ "And I will give you shepherds after My own heart, who will guide you with knowledge and understanding" (Jer. 3:15).

▪ "What sorrow awaits you shepherds who feed yourselves instead of your flocks. Shouldn't shepherds feed their sheep?" (Ez. 34:2).

▪ "Then the King will say to those on his right (sheep), 'Come, you who are blessed by my Father, inherit the Kingdom prepared for you from the creation of the world. For I was hungry, and you fed me. I was thirsty, and you gave me a drink. I was a stranger, and you invited me into your home. I was naked, and you gave me clothing. I was sick, and you cared for me. I was in prison, and you visited me'" (MATT. 25:34-36).

▪ "If a man has a hundred sheep and one of them wanders away, what will he do? Won't he leave the ninety-nine others on the hills and go out to search for the one that is lost? And if he finds it, I tell you the truth, he will rejoice over it more than over the ninety-nine that didn't wander away! In the same way, it is not my heavenly Father's will that even one of these little ones should perish" (MATT. 18:12-14).

✓ —— LIVING IN ALIGNMENT WITH THE GOOD SHEPHERD ——

☐ When will God stop looking for lost sheep? When God finds a lost sheep what does He do?
☐ What type of care are we to offer to the lost and hurting?
☐ What are the characteristics of a good shepherd?
☐ What am I doing to feed and care for disciples?
☐ How have I experienced God as my protector and provider?

FAITH IN ACTION: PRISON OUTREACH

▪ "I was in prison, and you visited Me."
▪ Discover a ministry in your city that has an outreach to a prison, or juvenile detention center. Plan a visit yourself or ask the ministry team what they need.

More ideas at GreatWithGod.com

Appeal to Heaven: Use the "R" You Praying Index to acknowledge Jesus as the The Good Shepherd. (Adapted from Ps. 23).

Sunday: Reflect. Lord Jesus, You are indeed my shepherd. You are not a hireling but You are my owner and I am valuable to You. You are indeed my shepherd; I shall not want.

Monday: Repent. I am so prone to stray. Do anything necessary to cause me to embrace a heart of continual repentance.

Tuesday: Rejoice. Jesus my shepherd, I give You thanks for Your goodness and provision. I rejoice for You make me to lie in green pastures. You lead me beside the still waters. You restore my soul.

Wednesday: Resist. Though I walk through the valley of the shadow of death I will fear no evil for You are with me. Your rod and Your staff protect me from my enemies. Deliver me from the wicked.

Thursday: Release. You prepare a table before me in the very presence of mine enemies. You anoint my head with oil. You have anointed me and prepared a place of ministry before me. Anoint me now to enter into Your work.

Friday: Recommit. Surely goodness and mercy shall follow me all the days of my life and I shall dwell in the house of the Lord forever. I recommit to encourage others to stay faithful to You.

Saturday: Receive. Good shepherd, train me to become a shepherd. Let's go together; You be the senior shepherd and I'll be the junior shepherd.

AMEN

GOD IS THE HOLY SPIRIT

FRUIT OF THE SPIRIT

PRAY USING VARIOUS PRAYER WHEEL INDEXES

YOUR GOAL: INCREASE YOUR INTIMACY WITH CHRIST. PRAYER IS TALKING TO GOD. USE THE VARIOUS PRAYER WHEEL INDEXES TO EXPAND YOUR VOCABULARY AND ADD DEPTH TO YOUR COMMUNICATION.

PRAYER WHEEL INDEX

You **can ask** for anything in my name,
and I will do it, so that the Son can
bring glory to the Father.

Jn. 14:13

START HERE

Love

The Image of God: "Beloved, let us love one another, for love is of God; and everyone who loves is born of God and knows God. He who does not love does not know God, for God is love. In this the love of God was manifested toward us, that God has sent His only begotten Son into the world, that we might live through Him. In this is love, not that we loved God, but that He loved us and sent His Son to be the propitiation for our sins" (1 Jn. 4:7-10).

▪ "Love suffers long and is kind; love does not envy; love does not parade itself, is not puffed up...; bears all things, believes all things, hopes all things, endures all things... And now abide faith, hope, love, these three, but the greatest of these is love" (1 Cor. 13:4, 7, 13).

▪ "For this is how God loved the world: He gave his one and only Son, so that everyone who believes in him will not perish but have eternal life" (Jn. 3:16).

— LOVE THE LORD —

The Command of Christ: "Jesus replied, 'The most important commandment is this: "Listen, O Israel! The Lord our God is the one and only Lord. And you must love the Lord your God with all your heart, all your soul, all your mind, and all your strength'''" (Mark 12:29-30).

▪ "If you love me, obey my commandments" (Jn. 14:15).

▪ "Those who accept my commandments and obey them are the ones who love me. And because they love me, my Father will love them. And I will love them and reveal myself to each of them" (Jn. 14:21).

▪ "There is no fear in love; but perfect love casts out fear, because fear involves torment"(1 Jn. 4:18).

- "I love those who love Me, and those who seek Me diligently will find Me" (Prov. 8:17).
- "I pray that from his glorious, unlimited resources he will empower you with inner strength through his Spirit. Then Christ will make his home in your hearts as you trust in him. Your roots will grow down into God's love and keep you strong. And may you have the power to understand, as all God's people should, how wide, how long, how high, and how deep his love is. May you experience the love of Christ, though it is too great to understand fully. Then you will be made complete with all the fullness of life and power that comes from God" (Eph. 3:16-19).

✓ —— LIVING IN ALIGNMENT WITH GOD'S LOVE ——

☐ Is there anything that keeps me from loving the Lord with all my heart, mind, soul and strength?
☐ What evidence is there that I am diligently pursuing a love relationship with God?
☐ Am I casting out fear from those around me?
☐ How can I show God that I love Him?
☐ How can I grow in patience and kindness?
☐ How can I remove envy and pride from life?

FAITH IN ACTION: LOVE YOUR MOM

- Be a blessing to your mother; send her a gift in the mail this week, with a nice note as to how she has benefited your life. Substitute a mentor if needed.

More ideas at GreatWithGod.com

"**AND SO**, dear brothers and sisters, I plead with You to give Your bodies to God because of all he has done for You. Let them be a living and holy sacrifice—the kind he will find acceptable. This is truly the way to worship him" (ROM. 12:1).

Heavenly Father, I present my body to You as a living and holy sacrifice. Come live through me, my body is now the temple of the Holy Spirit. Here are my **feet**; guide me where to go. Here are my **hands**; show me where to serve. Here is my **heart**; may Your may Your desires become mine. Here are my **eyes**; help me to see the world the way You see it. Here is my **mind**; renew it with Your truth. Here are my **ears**; help to hear the world the way You hear it. Here is my **mouth**; speak the truth in love through me. Amen. (See also 1 COR. 6:18-20).

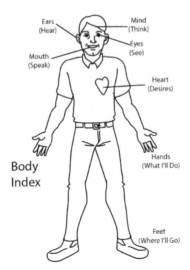

Ears (Hear)
Mind (Think)
Eyes (See)
Mouth (Speak)
Heart (Desires)
Hands (What I'll Do)

Body Index

Feet (Where I'll Go)

Appeal to Heaven: Pray using the **Body Index**. I present my body to God as a vessel of love.

Wisbit Tip: Touch each part of Your body as You dedicate it to God. Example, put Your hands on Your heart.

Sunday: Hands. I give You my hands (what I'll do). Use me today as a channel of Your love. I chose to serve. Cause me to see opportunities to serve others.

Monday: Feet. I give You my feet (where I'll go). Lead me and give me the grace to follow. Where I travel today belongs to You. Holy Spirit, let's go together.

Tuesday: Ears. I give You my ears; help me to hear the world the way You hear it. Help me to give the gift of listening to others today, especially the least and the lost.

Wednesday: Eyes. I give You my eyes (help me to see the world the way You see it). Help me to keep my mind pure by giving careful attention to what I watch and read. Give me eyes to see with compassion those who are in desperate need.

Thursday: Mouth. I give You my mouth; use me to speak words of life to those around me today. I give You my voice. Speak through me. Make me a voice of Your truth in both content and attitude.

Friday: Mind. I give You my mind; come be my teacher and interpret Your Scripture through the prism of Your love. Give me a spirit of understanding.

Saturday: Heart. I give You my heart. Please do whatever is necessary to change the desires of my heart to become a reflection of the desires in Your heart. Remake my heart in Your likeness. I present all of me as a living sacrifice to You.

Joy

The Image of God: "But the Holy Spirit produces this kind of fruit in our lives: love, joy, peace, patience, kindness, goodness, faithfulness…" (Gal. 5:22).

- "Thou wilt shew me the path of life: in thy presence is fulness of joy; at thy right hand there are pleasures for evermore" (Ps. 16:11 kjv).
- "In the same way, there is joy in the presence of God's angels when even one sinner repents" (Luke 15:10).
- "We do this by keeping our eyes on Jesus, the champion who initiates and perfects our faith. Because of the joy awaiting him, he endured the cross, disregarding its shame. Now he is seated in the place of honor beside God's throne" (Heb. 12:2).

— REJOICE —

The Command of Christ: "God blesses you when people mock you and persecute you and lie about you and say all sorts of evil things against you because you are my followers. Be happy about it! Be very glad! For a great reward awaits you in heaven. And remember, the ancient prophets were persecuted in the same way" (Matt. 5:11-12).

- "Always be joyful. Never stop praying. Be thankful in all circumstances, for this is God's will for you who belong to Christ Jesus" (1 Thes. 5:16-18).
- "Beloved, do not think it strange concerning the fiery trial which is to try you, as though some strange thing happened to you; but rejoice to the extent that you partake of Christ's sufferings, that when His glory is revealed, you may also be glad with exceeding joy" (2 Pet. 4:12-13).

- "Each time he said, 'My grace is all you need. My power works best in weakness.' So now I am glad to boast about my weaknesses, so that the power of Christ can work through me" (2 Cor. 12:9).
- "Dear brothers and sisters, when troubles of any kind come your way, consider it an opportunity for great joy. For you know that when your faith is tested, your endurance has a chance to grow. So let it grow, for when your endurance is fully developed, you will be perfect and complete, needing nothing" (Jam. 1:2-4).

✓   —— LIVING IN ALIGNMENT WITH GOD'S JOY ——

☐ Do I rejoice in my weaknesses?
☐ Do I thank God for my problems?
☐ Do I understand that God's way to greatness and glory comes when I rejoice at moments of adversity?
☐ Do I have true joy and not just happiness?
☐ Do I take comfort that God is both tester and defender?
☐ If I fail to rejoice in adversity, what is the outcome?
☐ Am I a vessel bringing joy to others? How?

FAITH IN ACTION: A SPOKEN BLESSING

- Verbally bless someone. Speak a word of encouragement. Say, "God is using you to encourage me. I see you becoming more and more a great leader for God. May God's grace cause you to grow into this destiny. Amen."

More ideas at GreatWithGod.com

"MY OLD SELF has been crucified with Christ. It is no longer I who live, but Christ lives in me. So I live in this earthly body by trusting in the Son of God, who loved me and gave himself for me" (GAL. 2:20).

Lord Jesus, I am not the **deliverer** but You are, and I am in You and You are in me. I can't **deliver** anyone but You can, and I am in You and You are in me. The truth, Lord, is that sometimes I don't want to **deliver** anyone, but You want to, and I am in You and You are in me. Lord, when it is all said and done I promise now, in advance, to give You all the credit because we both know the truth, I didn't **deliver** anyone but You did, because I was in You and You were in me. Lord, I yield myself to become a channel for the work of Your spirit. Amen.

Interchange the **Bold** words; example, Leader, Teacher.

The Four Spiritual Secrets Prayer Index

Secret 1	Secret 2	Secret 3	Secret 4
I'm not But You Are	I can't But You Can	I don't want to But You want to	I didn't But You did!

	Old Testament	New Testament
The Secrets Behind the 4 Secrets	I am with you and You are with me	I am in you and You are in me

The Secret to the Secrets	Full Surrender: Present your life to God as a living sacrifice.

Inspiration for the The Four Spiritual Secrets from Dick Woodward. Mini Bible College.[5]

APPEAL TO HEAVEN: Pray the **Four Spiritual Secrets** index to find joy by surrendering all.

SUNDAY: I AM NOT BUT YOU ARE. Heavenly Father, joy comes f rom resting in Your redemption, which is done through surrender. I confess the first secret that I am not sovereign but You are, and I am in You and You are in me.

MONDAY: I CAN'T BUT YOU CAN. Lord Almighty, joy comes f rom living for Your kingdom. Concerning Your kingdom, I confess the second secret that I can't deliver myself or anyone else but You can.

TUESDAY: I DON'T WANT TO BUT YOU WANT TO. Sovereign God, I know that joy comes f rom trusting You. But I admit the third secret: often I don't want to do Your will. Today I say not my will but Yours be done.

WEDNESDAY: I DIDN'T BUT YOU DID. Jesus, I praise You and acknowledge the fourth secret that You are working through my life. The successes I experience are not things I have done, but things that You have done.

THURSDAY: I AM WITH YOU AND YOU ARE WITH ME. Eternal God, joy comes from being in Your presence. The four spiritual secrets work because You are always with me. Help me to always be mindful that my identity is wrapped in the first secret: I'm not sovereign but You are.

FRIDAY: I AM IN YOU AND YOU ARE IN ME. Eternal God, I can't change others nor myself. But You are almighty and nothing is impossible with You. I am in You; You are in me.

SATURDAY: PROMISE TO GIVE GOD GLORY. Eternal God, I promise in advance to give You all the glory for the outcomes of my life and my prayers.

31

Peace

THE IMAGE OF GOD: "For He Himself is our peace, who has made both one, and has broken down the middle wall of separation, having abolished in His flesh the enmity, that is the law of commandments contained in ordinances, so as to create in Himself one new man from the two, thus making peace, and that He might reconcile them both to God in one body through the cross, thereby putting to death the enmity" (Eph. 2:14-16).

- "For unto us a Child is born, unto us a Son is given; And the government will be upon His shoulder, and His name shall be called Wonderful, Counselor, Mighty God, Everlasting Father, Prince of Peace" (Isa. 9:6-7).

- "Peace I leave with you, my peace I give unto you: not as the world giveth, give I unto you. Let not your heart be troubled, neither let it be afraid" (Jn. 14:27 KJV).

— HONOR MARRIAGE —

THE COMMAND OF CHRIST: "'Haven't you read the Scriptures?' Jesus replied. 'They record that from the beginning "God made them male and female." And he said, 'This explains why a man leaves his father and mother and is joined to his wife, and the two are united into one. Since they are no longer two but one, let no one split apart what God has joined together'" (MATT. 19:4-6).

- "In the same way, you husbands must give honor to your wives. Treat your wife with understanding as you live together. She may be weaker than you are, but she is your equal partner in God's gift of new life. Treat her as you should so your prayers will not be hindered" (1 PET. 3:7).

- "Don't worry about anything; instead, pray about everything. Tell God what you need, and thank him for all he has done. Then you will experience God's peace, which exceeds anything we can understand. His peace will guard your hearts and minds as you live in Christ Jesus" (PHIL. 4:6-7).
- "But the wisdom from above is first of all pure. It is also peace loving, gentle at all times, and willing to yield to others. It is full of mercy and the fruit of good deeds. It shows no favoritism and is always sincere. And those who are peacemakers will plant seeds of peace and reap a harvest of righteousness" (JAM. 3:17-18).

✓ — LIVING IN ALIGNMENT WITH THE PEACE OF GOD —

☐ Have I found peace with God?
☐ Am I at peace with all other people?
☐ What signs reveal that I have lost my peace?
☐ Do others view me as a peacemaker?
☐ Do I despise others for their immaturity?
☐ Can you remember a time when you experienced the peace of God in the midst of worldly calamity?
☐ What can you do to maintain peace of mind?
☐ How can I honor God's design for marriage?

FAITH IN ACTION: LETTER OF APPRECIATION

- The idea is to honor your spouse. Don't give a thank you card. Write a one page letter explaining how they have benefited your life. (If you're single, write to a dear friend or loved one.)

More ideas at GreatWithGod.com

"CAST ALL YOUR cares to God, for he cares for You" (1 PET. 5:7).

"Then Jesus said, 'Come to me, all of You who are weary and carry heavy burdens, and I will give You rest. Take my yoke upon You. Let me teach You, because I am humble and gentle at heart, and You will find rest'" (MATT. 11:28-29).

Heavenly Father, I thank You for Your invitation to cast my burdens upon You, for You care for me. I am weak and incapable. Lord Jesus, I yield to You now. I pray, not my will be done but Your will be done in my life. I transfer the ownership of all that I have to You. I dedicate all **my possessions**, all **my family**, all **my finances**, **my reputation**, **my schedule**, all **my rights** and all **my dreams**, to You. I'll give You thanks whatever happens. Amen.

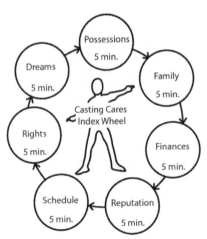

Inspiration for the Casting Cares Index from the Pineapple Series by Otto Koning.[6]

Appeal to Heaven: Use the **Casting Cares Index** to surrender every dimension of Your life to God and find peace.

Wisbit Tip: Kneel before an altar (make one) and voluntarily offer the various parts of Your life to God.

Sunday: My Possessions. "My things" now belong to You because I give them to You. Help me to be a faithful steward of all You allow me to keep. List and give your treasured possession to God one by one.

Monday: My Family. I entrust all my family to You. (List each member one by one). They are no longer mine. I can't worry about them anymore. I pray You keep them and bless them, for they are Yours. Use them for Your glory.

Tuesday: My Finances. My money is Your money. Show me how to be a good steward of the resources You put in my hands. Make me a funnel of Your resources. Give me the heart of a giver.

Wednesday: My Reputation. I will no longer live for my selfish ambition. I will no longer live to make my name great; from now on I live to make Your name great. My new goal is to guard and glorify Your reputation.

Thursday: My Schedule. All my time is Your time. I will not be angry when things don't go my way. My time is in your control, for You are sovereign. Order my steps today.

Friday: My Rights. You are not my servant, but today I acknowledge that I am Your servant. I want what You want. Thy will be done, thy kingdom come.

Saturday: My Dreams. I mean to offer my whole life to You; I'll do anything You want, anywhere You want, any time You want. At any cost, I'm all in. I'm Yours.

Patience

THE IMAGE OF GOD: "Now may the God of patience and comfort grant you to be like-minded toward one another, according to Christ Jesus, that you may with one mind and one mouth glorify the God and Father of our Lord Jesus Christ" (ROM. 15:5-6).

▪ "Don't you see how wonderfully kind, tolerant, and patient God is with you? Does this mean nothing to you? Can't you see that his kindness is intended to turn you from your sin?" (ROM. 2:4).

▪ "In the same way, even though God has the right to show his anger and his power, he is very patient with those on whom his anger falls..." (ROM. 9:22).

▪ "The Lord isn't really being slow about his promise, as some people think. No, he is being patient for your sake. He does not want anyone to be destroyed, but wants everyone to repent" (2 PET. 3:9).

—— WATCH AND PRAY ——

THE COMMAND OF CHRIST: "Keep watch and pray, so that you will not give in to temptation. For the spirit is willing, but the body is weak!" (MATT. 26:41).

▪ "Confess your sins to each other and pray for each other so that you may be healed. The earnest prayer of a righteous person has great power and produces wonderful results" (JAM. 5:16).

▪ "The temptations in your life are no different from what others experience. And God is faithful. He will not allow the temptation to be more than you can stand. When you are tempted, he will show you a way out so that you can endure" (1 COR. 10:13).

▪ "Dear friends, don't be surprised at the fiery trials you are going through, as if something strange were happening to you. Instead, be very glad—for these trials make you partners with Christ in his suffering, so that you will have the wonderful joy of seeing his glory when it is revealed to all the world. If you are insulted because you bear the name of Christ, you will be blessed, for the glorious Spirit of God rests upon you. If you suffer, however, it must not be for murder, stealing, making trouble, or prying into other people's affairs. But it is no shame to suffer for being a Christian. Praise God for the privilege of being called by his name!" (1 PET. 4:12-16).

✓ —— **LIVING IN ALIGNMENT WITH THE PATIENCE OF GOD** ——

☐ Do I welcome all suffering as trials allowed by God to refine my character?

☐ Am I routinely considerate of others by preferring their welfare above my own?

☐ Do I have good manners at all times, at all places, with all people?

☐ How can I prepare to withstand temptation?

☐ Do I appreciate the differences I find in others?

☐ When do I get impatient? What makes me angry?

FAITH IN ACTION: BLESS YOUR WAITER

▪ Pray for your waiter/waitress this week. As they deliver your food, say, "It's my custom to pray before each meal. Is there something I could pray for you about?" Pray and leave a generous tip.

More ideas at GreatWithGod.com

"BE THANKFUL in all circumstances, for this is God's will for You who belong to Christ Jesus" (1 THES. 5:18).

Heavenly Father, Jehovah Jireh, I pause to recognize that every good and perfect gift that has come to me was through You and because of You. The world is sustained by You. My breath is Your provision. Thank You for the many **answered prayers**. What is it that I have that You have not provided? My **salvation** and everything about me—my **talents, spiritual gifts, body,** and **family** are all Your design. Even through **my suffering** You are causing all things to work together for my good. Thank You for my **mentors** who help me understand that every weakness is a blessing in disguise. Therefore, I pause today to say thank You. Amen.

Count Your Blessings Ledger Index	
Index	Get Specific
Family	
Personal Traits, Talents, Skills, Size, Mind	
Salvation	
Provision	
Glory in Weakness	
Spiritual Gifts	
Teacher / Mentor	
ANSWERED PRAYER	

APPEAL TO HEAVEN: Use the **Count Your Blessings Ledger Index** as You acknowledge the patience of God.

WISBIT TIP: Start a prayer log. Record request and answers.

SUNDAY: FAMILY. Heavenly Father, I often approach You asking for help for my every need. Today I pause to say thank You for my family (Mom, Dad, brothers, sisters) as I count my blessings.

MONDAY: DESIGN LORD JESUS. I realize I am Your custom design. You've equipped me exactly to fulfill my mission. I praise You for I am wonderfully made.

TUESDAY: SALVATION. I thank You for adopting me into Your family and for writing my name in the book of life. Thank You for eternal life. Thank You for dying in my place. I purpose now to live life with a grateful spirit.

WEDNESDAY: PROVISION. I am alive because of Your continuous provision. Thank You for my every breath, drink, meal and paycheck. These ultimately come from You. I recognize You as my provider.

THURSDAY: GLORY IN WEAKNESS. I even thank You for my weaknesses. Your strength is made perfect in weakness, and all things are working together for the good of those who love You and are pursuing living for Your purpose.

FRIDAY: SPIRITUAL GIFTS. I thank You for my unique spiritual gift. I realize we all need each other and I celebrate the diversity of the church. Help me to fulfill my role.

SATURDAY: TEACHERS. Today I am thankful for the many mentors/teachers that have added so much value to me over the years. I am the person I am today because of these people of influence in my life.

Kindness

THE IMAGE OF GOD: "The Holy Spirit produces this kind of fruit in our lives: love, joy, peace, patience, kindness, goodness, faithfulness…" (GAL. 5:22).

■ "That in the ages to come He might show the exceeding riches of His grace in His kindness toward us in Christ Jesus" (EPH. 2:7).

■ "Notice how God is both kind and severe. He is severe toward those who disobeyed, but kind to you if you continue to trust in his kindness. But if you stop trusting, you also will be cut off" (ROM. 11:22).

■ "And since it is through God's kindness, then it is not by their good works. For in that case, God's grace would not be what it really is—free and undeserved" (ROM. 11:6).

— GO THE SECOND MILE —

THE COMMAND OF CHRIST: "You have heard the law that says the punishment must match the injury: 'An eye for an eye, and a tooth for a tooth.' But I say, do not resist an evil person! If someone slaps you on the right cheek, offer the other cheek also. If you are sued in court and your shirt is taken from you, give your coat, too. If a soldier demands that you carry his gear for a mile, carry it two miles. Give to those who ask, and don't turn away from those who want to borrow" (MATT. 5:38-41).

■ "Dear friends, never take revenge. Leave that to the righteous anger of God. For the Scriptures say, 'I will take revenge; I will pay them back,' says the Lord. Instead, if your enemies are hungry, feed them. If they are thirsty, give them something to drink…Don't let evil conquer you, but conquer evil by doing good" (ROM. 12:19-21).

▪ "Give, and you will receive. Your gift will return to you in full—pressed down, shaken together to make room for more, running over, and poured into your lap. The amount you give will determine the amount you get back" (LUKE 6:38).

▪ "If you help the poor, you are lending to the LORD and he will repay you!" (PROV. 19:17).

▪ "If you love only those who love you, what reward is there for that? Even corrupt tax collectors do that much" (MATT. 5:46).

✓ ─── LIVING IN ALIGNMENT WITH THE KINDNESS OF GOD ───

☐ Do I care enough about those near to me to make my gifts to them personalized and considerate?

☐ Do I give to others even when I cannot be repaid?

☐ Do I return good when evil is done to me?

☐ Have I forsaken every form of revenge?

☐ Do I look for ways to benefit others?

☐ Other than gifts in what ways can I show kindness to others?

☐ Do I show favoritism with whom I show kindness?

☐ Does my kindness extend to those from foreign cultures?

FAITH IN ACTION: AT-WORK KINDNESS INITIATIVE

▪ Simply do a chore on someone else's things to-do list: run an errand, mail delivery, declutter the breakroom, clean out the refrigerator. One example is to wash and vacuum a colleague's car. Use wisdom but try not to ask permission; just initiate and do kindness.

More ideas at GreatWithGod.com

A **POINT** of contact is something that You do as You pray to help You stir up and release Your faith. Jesus modeled this when he spat on the ground, made mud, and applied it onto the eyelids of a blind man who washed it off, was healed and could see.

Creator of the universe, You are the God of all creativity. Your Holy Spirit accomplishes Your work in the earth. Let the Holy Spirit's creativity be expressed in and through me. Increase my faith. Help me to discern what You are doing so I can join You. Nothing is impossible with You. I believe that putting faith into action (sometime through a point of contact) is the very catalyst that may please You and release Your kingdom on earth. Teach me and guide me how to ignite my faith with Point of Contact action prayer.

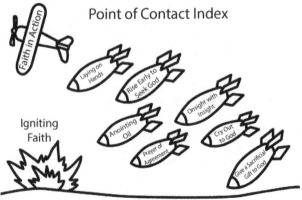

Point of Contact Index

Faith in Action

Igniting Faith

Laying on Hands

Rise Early to Seek God

Onsight with Insight

Anointing Oil

Prayer of Agreement

Cry Out to God

Give a Sacrificial Gift to God

A Symbolic Action Accompanying Prayer

Inspiration for the Point of Contact Index from the preaching of Oral Roberts.[7]

Appeal to Heaven: Ask God to manifest kindness through His servants.

Wisbit Tip: Use **Points of Contact** to pray actively by making use of a thing, activity or a symbol to add fervency to prayer, stir up faith and unleash God's power.

Sunday: Laying on of Hands and the Outstretched Arm. Activate faith by laying Your hands on those for whom You are praying.

Monday: Cry Out to God. Vocalize Your desperation. Ask God to make You a channel of His kindness.

Tuesday: On Sight with Insight. Go to one of the places where an event will be held and pray at that location, asking God to reveal Himself to the people who come there. (This is the idea behind the Jericho Prayer Walks).

Wednesday: Prayer of Agreement. Add fervency by agreeing with another believer in prayer. Ask God to meet their most pressing need in Jesus' name.

Thursday: Anointing Oil. Anointing oil is a symbol of the Holy Spirit. Apply anointing oil to places and lives where You sense God leading. Pray, "Holy Spirit, You are welcome here."

Friday: Give a Sacrificial Gift for God. Add fervency to Your prayers by giving a sacrificial gift to a church or ministry. Pray, "God, I give to honor Your name. I give in faith to release and resource kingdom work."

Saturday: Rising Early. Add fervency to Your prayers by rising earlier than usual, 15 minutes to an hour. With that time, do a prayer walk through Your neighborhood. Ask God how You could show Your neighbors His kindness.

34

Goodness

THE IMAGE OF GOD: "Once a religious leader asked Jesus this question: 'Good Teacher, what should I do to inherit eternal life?' 'Why do you call me good?' Jesus asked him. 'Only God is truly good'"(LUKE 18:18-19).

▪ "Surely your goodness and unfailing love will pursue me all the days of my life, and I will live in the house of the Lord forever" (Ps. 23:6).

▪ "How great is the goodness you have stored up for those who fear you. You lavish it on those who come to you for protection, blessing them before the watching world" (Ps. 31:19).

▪ "And do you think this, O man, you who judge those practicing such things, and doing the same that you will escape the judgment of God? Or do you despise the riches of His goodness, forbearance, and long-suffering, not knowing that the goodness of God leads you to repentance?" (ROM. 2:3-4)

— BRING IN THE POOR —

THE COMMAND OF CHRIST: "Then he turned to his host. 'When you put on a luncheon or a banquet,' he said, 'don't invite your f riends, brothers, relatives, and rich neighbors. For they will invite you back, and that will be your only reward. Instead, invite the poor, the crippled, the lame, and the blind. Then at the resurrection of the righteous, God will reward you for inviting those who could not repay you'" (LUKE 14:12-14).

▪ "Give justice to the poor and the orphan; uphold the rights of the oppressed and the destitute. Rescue the poor and helpless; deliver them from the grasp of evil people" (Ps. 82:3-4).

- "If you help the poor, you are lending to the LORD and he will repay you!" (PROV. 19:17).
- "Blessed are those who are generous, because they feed the poor" (Prov. 22:9).
- "Whoever gives to the poor will lack nothing, but those who close their eyes to poverty will be cursed" (PROV. 28:27).
- "And I have been a constant example of how you can help those in need by working hard. You should remember the words of the Lord Jesus: 'It is more blessed to give than to receive'" (ACTS 20:35).

✓ —— LIVING IN ALIGNMENT WITH GOD' GOODNESS ——

☐ Do you plan creative ways to bless others?
☐ Are your motives filled with the idea of adding value to others?
☐ Do you seek opportunities to help others?
☐ Do you have prejudices that limit your goodness?
☐ Do you repay good for evil?
☐ Is your heart pure in your motives in pursuing God?
☐ Do I see myself as an agent of God's goodness, kindness and freedom?

FAITH IN ACTION: BE A FREEDOM AGENT

- Allow God to defend, serve, deliver, and provide for widows and orphans, through you as his agent. **Play Defense**: take a stand for righteousness and find a solution that protects and delivers widows and orphans from injustice. Write a justice solution letter to those responsible for correcting oppression and injustice.

More ideas at GreatWithGod.com

Hear The Mission of Christ: "The Spirit of the Lord is upon Me, Because He has anointed Me to preach the gospel to the poor; He has sent Me to heal the broken-hearted, To proclaim liberty to the captives And recovery of sight to the blind, To set at liberty those who are oppressed; To proclaim the acceptable year of the Lord" (cf Luke 4:18).

Hear Jesus Commission to his disciples: (Jn. 20:21).

MISSION OF CHRIST Index stairs

5 min. Give Life

5 min. Preach Jubilee

5 min. Set at Liberty the Bruised

5 min. Recovery of Sight

5 min. Deliverance to the Captives

5 min. Heal the Broken Hearted

5 min. Preach the Gospel to the Poor

APPEAL TO HEAVEN: Use the **Mission of Christ Index** to add fervency to Your prayers by aligning with His work.

WISBIT TIP: Let God use You to answer Your prayers for others by finding a practical way to serve others.

SUNDAY: PREACH THE GOSPEL TO THE POOR. Heavenly Father, I come boldly before You today to ask You to raise up laborers, evangelists and prophets to preach the gospel to the poor. Here I am Lord, send me.

MONDAY: HEAL THE BROKEN-HEARTED. Holy Spirit, raise up godly Christian counselors who will speak Your truth with compassion to those who are indeed broken hearted. Use me as a channel of You truth and love.

TUESDAY: DELIVERANCE TO THE CAPTIVES. Lord Jesus, raise up laborers, great in faith, to preach deliverance to those who are in bondage to evil. Lord, prepare and send me. Anoint me. Make me an agent of Your freedom.

WEDNESDAY: RECOVERY OF SIGHT TO THE BLIND. God, You are the Great Physician. I ask You to raise up doctors and nurses to work in Your name. Send Your team of healers to the very ends of the earth.

THURSDAY: SET AT LIBERTY THE BRUISED. Lord, send deliverance to those who are enslaved. Raise up ministries to deliver children from sex trafficking.

FRIDAY: PREACH THE ACCEPTABLE YEAR OF THE LORD. Today I pray not that You would raise up others but that You would prepare and send me.

SATURDAY: GIVE PEOPLE ABUNDANT LIFE. Father, I pray that You will empower me with inner strength through Your Spirit to do Your work on earth.

35 *Faithfulness*

THE IMAGE OF GOD: "The fruit of the Spirit is... Faithfulness..." (GAL. 5:22).

▪ "Your mercy, O Lord, is in the heavens; Your faithfulness reaches to the clouds. Your righteousness is like the great mountains; Your judgments are a great deep; O Lord, You preserve man and beast" (Ps. 36:5-6).

▪ "And from Jesus Christ, the faithful witness, the firstborn from the dead, and the ruler over the kings of the earth. To Him who loved us and washed us from our sins in His own blood" (REV. 1:5).

▪ "O Lord God of Heaven's Armies! Where is there anyone as mighty as you, O Lord? You are entirely faithful" (Ps. 89:8).

— DENY YOURSELF —

THE COMMAND OF CHRIST: "Then he said to the crowd, 'If any of you wants to be my follower, you must give up your own way, take up your cross daily, and follow me. If you try to hang on to your life, you will lose it. But if you give up your life for my sake, you will save it. And what do you benefit if you gain the whole world but are yourself lost or destroyed?'" (LUKE 9:23-25).

▪ "My old self has been crucified with Christ. It is no longer I who live, but Christ lives in me. So I live in this earthly body by trusting in the Son of God, who loved me and gave himself for me" (GAL. 2:20).

▪ "Yes, everything else is worthless when compared with the infinite value of knowing Christ Jesus my Lord. For his sake I have discarded everything else, counting it all as garbage, so that I could gain Christ" (PHIL. 3:8).

- "Soldiers don't get tied up in the affairs of civilian life, for then they cannot please the officer who enlisted them" (2 Tɪᴍ. 2:4).
- "...put on every piece of God's armor so you will be able to resist the enemy in the time of evil. Then...Stand your ground, putting on the belt of truth and the breastplate of God's righteousness. For shoes, put on the peace that comes from the Good News....hold up the shield of faith to stop the fiery arrows of the devil. Put on salvation as your helmet, and take the sword of the Spirit, which is the word of God. Pray in the Spirit at all times and on every occasion. Stay alert and be persistent in your prayers ..." (Eᴘʜ. 6:13-18)

✓ — LIVING IN ALIGNMENT WITH THE FAITHFULNESS OF GOD —

- ☐ How do you demonstrate faithfulness?
- ☐ Can you remember a trial when you wanted to quit and yet you remained faithful? Why?
- ☐ Who can you think of who remained faithful during a trial?
- ☐ What answers to prayer do I have of Gods power?
- ☐ Do I patiently trust in the Lords faithfulness even when my prayers don't get answered immediately?
- ☐ How can I honor those who are faithful?

FAITH IN ACTION: BLESS A MINISTER

- Bless a pastor or other ministry worker this week. Take them to lunch or breakfast. Honor them with a gift, note, call or visit.

More ideas at GreatWithGod.com

PUT ON THE FULL ARMOR OF GOD

LORD JESUS, I call myself to a readiness of mind. My feet are **shod** with the gospel; everywhere I travel, I am an ambassador of the gospel. I put on the **belt** of truth reminding myself that Your word is true and trustworthy. I put on the **breastplate** of righteousness and declare the blood of Jesus Christ continually cleanses me from all my sin. I wear the **helmet** of salvation for I have been born of the spirit and adopted into Your family. My **shield** of faith is made steadfast by identifying with the power of God and not my own strength. His victory enables my victory over every temptation. I train myself to skillfully handle the **sword** of the word. I will not quit. I will advance the gospel. In Jesus name, I **stand**.

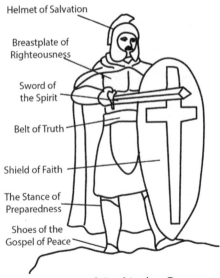

Helmet of Salvation

Breastplate of Righteousness

Sword of the Spirit

Belt of Truth

Shield of Faith

The Stance of Preparedness

Shoes of the Gospel of Peace

The Armor of God Index Prayer

APPEAL TO HEAVEN: Use the **Armor of God Index** to add fervency to Your prayers.

WISBIT TIP: Pray Scriptures. Consider using God's Names, Commands & Promises listed in this book.

SUNDAY: BELT OF TRUTH. Increase my faith. Faith comes by hearing the word of God. Holy Spirit, guide me into truth. As I read the Scriptures, give me a spirit of understanding.

MONDAY: BREASTPLATE OF RIGHTEOUSNESS. The blood of Jesus Christ continually cleanses me from all my sins. I am eternally forgiven of all my sins, past present and future. I am righteous in the blood of Christ.

TUESDAY: SHOES PREPARED TO SHARE GOSPEL OF PEACE. Lord, make me a soul winner. Cause my life to proclaim the gospel of salvation. Help me share Your love.

WEDNESDAY: SHIELD OF FAITH. Lord, I pray as did Your disciples: increase my faith. Give me a revelation knowledge of the nature of Jesus Christ. I trust in Your unchanging nature and Your unchanging word.

THURSDAY: HELMET OF SALVATION. Lord God, right now I rededicate my life to Christ. Forgive me and adopt me into Your family. Write my name in the book of life.

FRIDAY: SWORD OF THE SPIRIT, WHICH IS THE WORD OF GOD. Let Your word guide my mind so I can take every thought captive and bring it under the Lordship of Christ.

SATURDAY: STANCE OF PREPAREDNESS; THE BATTLE CRY OF SCRIPTURE-FED, SPIRIT-LED, PROMISE-BASED PRAYER. With a heart and mind prepared with the full armor of God, Lord, give me courage to stand up and speak up.

Gentleness

THE IMAGE OF GOD: "You have also given me the shield of Your salvation; Your gentleness has made me great. You enlarged my path under me; so my feet did not slip" (2 SAM. 22:36-37).

▪ "Now I, Paul, appeal to you with the gentleness and kindness of Christ—though I realize you think I am timid in person and bold only when I write from far away" (2 COR. 10:1).

▪ "But the fruit of the spirit is... gentleness..." (GAL. 5:22-23).

▪ "But the wisdom from above is first of all pure. It is also peace loving, gentle at all times, and willing to yield to others. It is full of mercy and the fruit of good deeds. It shows no favoritism and is always sincere" (JAM. 3:17).

— HEAR GOD'S VOICE —

THE COMMAND OF CHRIST: "Anyone with ears to hear should listen and understand!" (MATT. 11:15).

▪ "So faith comes from hearing, that is, hearing the Good News about Christ" (ROM. 10:17).

▪ "When the Spirit of truth comes, he will guide you into all truth. He will not speak on his own but will tell you what he has heard. He will tell you about the future" (JN. 16:13).

▪ "My sheep listen to my voice; I know them, and they follow me" (JN. 10:27).

▪ "I will bless the Lord who guides me; even at night my heart instructs me" (Ps.16:7).

▪ "And if someone asks about your hope as a believer, always be ready to explain it. But do this in a gentle and
respectful way. Keep your conscience clear. Then if people
speak against you, they will be ashamed when they see
what a good life you live because you belong to Christ"
(1 PET. 3:15-16).

▪ "A gentle answer deflects anger, but harsh words make
tempers flare" (PROV. 15:1).

✓ ─── LIVING IN ALIGNMENT WITH THE GENTLENESS OF GOD ───

☐ Do I do my daily tasks in an attitude of gentleness?
☐ Are my words soft when addressing others?
☐ How can I express gentleness to family and friends?
☐ Am I quick to listen and slow to speak?
☐ Do I try and see life from the other person's point of view?
☐ Am I aware of the different types of needs of those
   around me?
☐ Am I sensitive to the wishes of others, especially
   when they want things done a certain way?

FAITH IN ACTION: BLESS A FIRST RESPONDER

▪Go to your local fire station. Say to the firemen,
"Thank you for being quick to respond to the cries for
help throughout this district. God is using you to save
lives. I would like to say thank you in a practical way,
so here's a little snack/gift. I wanted to be a blessing to
the team. Risking your lives to save lives is Christlike.
I can never say thank you enough."

More ideas at GreatWithGod.com

"Come and listen to my counsel. I'll share my heart with you and make you wise" (PROV. 1:23).

Ask God Questions and Listen For His Response:

Write your prayers, questions and His answers. This is called dialogue journaling. You will be having a conversation with God, spirit to spirit. The very mind of God communicating with your mind in your mind. Write down the questions and write down what you perceive as His answers. Just write first and evaluate what was written later. Learning to listen is half of the equation to dynamic faith in God.

LISTENING PRAYER

*This Dialogue Journal Index was inspired and adapted
from the Radical Mentoring, Letter From God.*[8]

APPEAL TO HEAVEN: Pray using the Listening Prayer: Dialogue Journaling Index. This particular listening index was modeled after the pattern of Jesus' letters written to His churches listed in Revelation, Chapters 2-3.

WISBIT TIP: Ask God questions (write the questions as well) and write down what comes to your mind.

SUNDAY: IDENTITY. Heavenly Father, my creator, Who am I? Who have You made me to be? What work do You want me to do?

MONDAY: AFFIRMATION. Jehovah Roi, You are the God who sees everything. What am I doing well?

TUESDAY: REBUKE. Holy Righteous Judge of the universe speak to me and help me see where I need to repent. What do You hold against me?

WEDNESDAY: CHALLENGE. God of all grace, give me the power to change. What do You want me to do to correct this area of rebuke?

THURSDAY: CONSEQUENCES. God Almighty, You are sovereign over all the world and the all the affairs of men; tell me the consequences if I do not respond to this challenge You have given to me?

FRIDAY: REWARD. Jehovah Jireh, You are my provider. Every good thing in my life has come through Your provision; what reward now awaits me if I respond to this challenge?

SATURDAY: SIGNATURE. Yahweh, the Great I Am, which of Your names is in alignment with the faith steps You are asking of me?

SPIRIT FRUIT

Self-Control

The Image of God: "But the Holy Spirit produces this kind of fruit in our lives: love, joy, peace, patience, kindness, goodness, faithfulness, gentleness and self-control. There is no law against these things!" (Gal. 5:22-23).

▪ "But, beloved, do not forget this one thing, that with the Lord one day is as a thousand years, and a thousand years as one day. The Lord is not slack concerning His promise, as some count slackness, but is long-suffering toward us, not willing that any should perish but that all should come to repentance" (2 Pet. 3:8-9).

▪ "...keeping our eyes on Jesus, the champion who initiates and perfects our faith. Because of the joy awaiting him, he endured the cross, disregarding its shame. Now he is seated in the place of honor beside God's throne" (Heb. 12:2).

— SECRET DISCIPLINES —

The Command of Christ: "But when you give to someone in need, don't let your left hand know what your right hand is doing. Give your gifts in private, and your Father, who sees everything, will reward you...But when you pray, go away by yourself, shut the door behind you, and pray to your Father in private. Then your Father, who sees everything, will reward you...But when you fast, comb your hair and wash your face. Then no one will notice that you are fasting, except your Father, who knows what you do in private. And your Father, who sees everything, will reward you" (Matt. 6:3-4,6, 17-18)." "...Instead, train yourself to be godly"(1 Tim. 4:7).

GOD'S PROMISES: TO ALL WHO PRACTICE SELF-CONTROL (FASTING) TO BE BLESSED

■ "Then your salvation will come like the dawn, and your wounds will quickly heal. Your godliness will lead you forward, and the glory of the LORD will protect you from behind. Then when you call, the LORD will answer. 'Yes, I am here,' he will quickly reply…Feed the hungry, and help those in trouble. Then your light will shine…you will be as bright as noon" (Is. 58:8-10).

■ "Rather, he must enjoy having guests in his home, and he must love what is good. He must live wisely and be just. He must live a devout and disciplined life. He must have a strong belief in the trustworthy message he was taught; then he will be able to encourage others with wholesome teaching and show those who oppose it where they are wrong" (Titus 1:8-9).

✓ ─── LIVING IN ALIGNMENT WITH THE FRUIT OF SELF CONTROL ───

☐ What's the difference between self-control and patience?

☐ How can I measure my personal levels of self-control?

☐ Am I regularly practicing the spiritual disciplines of giving to others and to God, of praying, of fasting?

☐ When was the last time I fasted for a day, three days, a full week, 21 days, 40 days?

☐ What if I fail to grow in self-control?

☐ How can I cultivate self-control in my life?

FAITH IN ACTION: FASTING

■ Your assignment is to fast one meal every day this work week. Replace the time you would spend eating with prayer focused on helping the oppressed. Thursday add action to prayer by giving a meal.

More ideas at GreatWithGod.com

"Howbeit this kind goeth not out but by prayer and fasting" (MATT. 17:21 KJV).

"...This is the kind of fasting I want: Free those who are wrongly imprisoned; lighten the burden of those who work for You. Let the oppressed go free, and remove the chains that bind people. Share Your food with the hungry, and give shelter to the homeless. Give clothes to those who need them, and do not hide from relatives who need Your help" (Is. 58:6-7 NLT).

God whose nature is freedom, I come to You with prayer and fasting today. Deliver us from evil and deliver us from the evil one. Let Your kingdom come and undo the effects of sin and wickedness. Today I pray and fast that the things that break Your heart would break my heart. Use me as Your vessel to bring freedom to the enslaved, justice to the oppressed, practical help to the poor and reconciliation to those estranged from You. Amen.

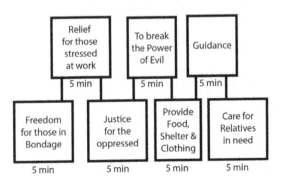

Fasting Index for Provision, Freedom, Deliverance
Justice, Relief and Direction

Appeal to Heaven: Pray using **Isaiah 58, God's Purpose for Fasting Index**.

Wisbit Tip: Add fervency and power to Your prayers by coupling them with times of fasting.

Sunday: Freedom for Those in Bondage. Lord God, whose very nature is freedom, I fast today asking that You deliver those have been wrongfully imprisoned.

Monday: Relief for Those Stressed at Work. Lord, I fast today that all employers around the world would show compassion upon their employees. Give the rest You promised to those who come to You.

Tuesday: Justice for the Oppressed. I call out aloud to You with fasting to bring liberty to those who are in bondage to sin and to Satan. Send forth laborers to make manifest the rule of Your kingdom.

Wednesday: To Break the Power of Evil. The truth will set You free. There are physical chains and there are inner wounds of the heart and mind that also bind lives. Today I fast to set all captives free.

Thursday: Provide Food and Shelter. You have prayed; now is the time to do. Take Your meal that You fasted and give it to someone else or buy someone else a meal.

Friday: Provide Clothing. Consider this a bonus assignment. Go into Your closet and choose clothes that You will distribute to those in need. Get creative, but get it done.

Saturday: Care for Relatives in Need. Don't reach out to the world and neglect those who are closest to You. Pray intelligently for Your family by asking for their prayer requests. Offer practical assistance to help meet their needs.

God the Holy Spirit

The Sevenfold Spirit

Pray Using the Ripple Prayer Index

Your Goal: Pray through the Ripple Intercession Prayer each day. Then pray for 5 minutes concerning the index theme assigned each day. Use the prayer guide at the end of each chapter to help you get started.

On Saturday, complete your meditation for the week by praying completely through the Ripple Prayer Index in 35 minutes.

Wisbit Tip: Increase prayer power by joining with other believers to pray together in a spirit of agreement. Have an agreement prayer gathering at a strategic location

THE RIPPLE INTERCESSION INDEX PRAYER

"THE SPIRIT OF THE LORD will rest on him—the Spirit of wisdom and understanding, the Spirit of counsel and might, the Spirit of knowledge and the fear of the Lord" (Is. 11:2).

Lord Jesus, have mercy on those You have created; I know that it is Your desire that none should perish but that all should come to eternal life. Grant **parents** a spirit of wisdom. Bless **pastors** with a spirit of understanding. Give **school administrators** a spirit of counsel. Grant our **city police** and **justice officials** a spirit of might. Let a spirit of knowledge rest upon on our **state legislators**. Bless our **president, Supreme Court,** and **representatives** with the spirit of the fear of the Lord. I ask the Holy Spirit to raise up laborers to do the work of disciple-making for **every nation** and **tribe.** Amen.

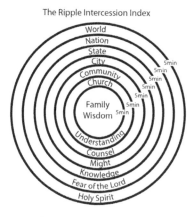

The Ripple Intercession Index

Inspiration for the Ripple Index from Dr. David Yonggi Cho. Learn How to Pray Tabernacle Prayer.[9]

Spirit of Wisdom

THE IMAGE OF GOD: "God has united you with Christ Jesus. For our benefit God made Him to be wisdom itself. Christ made us right with God: He made us pure and holy, and He freed us from sin" (1 COR. 1:30).

▪ "But the wisdom that is from above is first pure, then peaceable, gentle, willing to yield, full of mercy and good fruits, without partiality and without hypocrisy" (JAS. 3:17).

▪ "I have filled him with the Spirit of God, giving him great wisdom, ability, and expertise in all kinds of crafts" (EX. 31:3).

▪ "And the Spirit of the Lord will rest on him—the Spirit of wisdom and understanding, the Spirit of counsel and might, the Spirit of knowledge and the fear of the Lord" (Is. 11:2).

— BE WISE AS SERPENTS —

THE COMMAND OF CHRIST: "Look, I am sending you out as sheep among wolves. So be as shrewd as snakes and harmless as doves" (MATT. 10:16).

▪ "The fear of the Lord is the beginning of Wisdom; A good understanding have all those who do His commandments. His praise endures forever" (Ps. 111:10).

▪ "Wisdom is the principle thing; therefore get wisdom. And in all your getting, get understanding. Exalt her, and she will promote you; She will bring you honor, when you embrace her" (PROV. 4:7-8).

▪ "If you need wisdom, ask our generous God, and he will give it to you. He will not rebuke you for asking" (JAM. 1:5).

▪ "A spiritual gift is given to each of us so we can help each other. To one person the Spirit gives the ability to give wise advice; to another the same Spirit gives a message of special knowledge. The same Spirit gives great faith to another, and to someone else the one Spirit gives the gift of healing. He gives one person the power to perform miracles, and another the ability to prophesy. He gives someone else the ability to discern whether a message is from the Spirit of God or from another spirit. Still another person is given the ability to speak in unknown languages, while another is given the ability to interpret what is being said" (1 COR. 12:7-10).

✓ —— LIVING IN ALIGNMENT WITH THE SPIRIT OF WISDOM ——

☐ What if I don't ask God to give me wisdom?
☐ What does it mean, wisdom is willing to yield?
☐ What does prejudice and stubbornness reveal?
☐ How aware am I that God is evaluating my every thought, word and deed?
☐ Where does wisdom come from?
☐ What's the difference between worldly wisdom and Godly wisdom?

FAITH IN ACTION: THROUGH WISDOM GIVE WISDOM

▪ Send a wise thought, a proverb, a Scripture, through a note, email, text, etc. For example, send a Scripture from this page of Scriptures. Choose one and send it to someone who may consider it a timely blessing. Carefully consider whom you will encourage. Through wisdom give wisdom.

More ideas at GreatWithGod.com

APPEAL TO HEAVEN: Using the **Ripple Intercession Index** prayer, focus on the Spirit of Wisdom and the manifestational gifts of the spirit (1 COR. 12:7-11)

SUNDAY: FAMILY. Spirit of wisdom, come fill my family. You said You give wisdom to those who ask. I ask that You would give me a wise and understanding heart. Guide me into all wisdom. Holy Spirit, be my teacher now and always.

MONDAY: CHURCH. Lord God, thank You for the pastors who serve at my church. Bless them with a spirit of wisdom. Grant them spiritual discernment and knowledge as they counsel others.

TUESDAY: COMMUNITY. www.blesseveryhome.com. Go to this website and register today. They will then send You a list of Your nearest neighbors so You can pray for them by name. Ask God to bless them with wisdom from above.

WEDNESDAY: CITY. Lord of the harvest, today I pray for my city, that You would raise up more pastors, small group leaders, and mentors. Manifest the gift of faith and miracles through these laborers.

THURSDAY: STATE. The word of God teaches us that prayers and intercessions should be made on behalf of our government leaders (list names). Give them wisdom and manifest the gift of healing to the families of these leaders.

FRIDAY: NATION. I pray for the Jewish people and the nation of Israel today. Give them wisdom and the ability to discern spirits so they can see Jesus as Messiah.

SATURDAY: WORLD. Father, raise up leaders and grant them wise strategies to bring this gospel to every nation and manifest the gift of prophecy in their ministries.

39 Spirit of Understanding

THE IMAGE OF GOD: "And the Spirit of the LORD will rest on Him—the Spirit of wisdom and understanding, the Spirit of counsel and might, the Spirit of knowledge and the fear of the LORD" (Is. 11:2).

▪ "By wisdom the Lord founded the earth; by understanding he created the heavens" (PROV. 3:19).

▪ "But true wisdom and power are found in God; counsel and understanding are his" (JOB. 12:13).

▪ "Give me an understanding heart so that I can govern your people well and know the difference between right and wrong. For who by himself is able to govern this great people of yours?" (1 CHRON. 1:10).

— DO NOT CAST PEARLS —

THE COMMAND OF CHRIST: "Don't waste what is holy on people who are unholy. Don't throw your pearls to pigs! They will trample the pearls, then turn and attack you" (MATT. 7:6).

▪ "Guard your heart above all else, for it determines the course of your life" (PROV. 4:23).

▪ "So I want you to know that no one speaking by the Spirit of God will curse Jesus, and no one can say Jesus is Lord, except by the Holy Spirit" (1 COR. 12:3).

▪ "Leave your simple ways behind, and begin to live; learn to use good judgment. Anyone who rebukes a mocker will get an insult in return. Anyone who corrects the wicked will get hurt. So don't bother correcting mockers; they will only hate you. But correct the wise, and they will love you" (PROV. 9:6-8).

▪ "To those who listen to My teaching, more understanding will be given, and they will have an abundance of knowledge. But for those who are not listening, even what little understanding they have will be taken away from them" (MATT. 13:12).

▪ "But when the Father sends the Advocate as My representative—that is, the Holy Spirit—He will teach you everything and will remind you of everything I have told you" (JN. 14:16).

✓— LIVING IN ALIGNMENT WITH THE SPIRIT OF UNDERSTANDING —

☐ Am I discerning on who I share spiritual truth with?
☐ Whom should I avoid? Whom should I seek to share truth with?
☐ What are the characteristics of spiritual pigs and dogs?
☐ What are characteristics of a man of understandings?
☐ How can I cultivate a heart for obedience?
☐ How can I guard my heart?
☐ Am I quick to obey the promptings of the Holy Spirit?

FAITH IN ACTION: LEND A DVD

▪ Wisely lend a DVD of The Case for Christ with someone you think will appreciate it. Do not give to a scoffer. This assignment is the opposite of throwing pearls to swine. It's equipping the hungry for more of God. Lend, not give. Ask for it back in 10 days and discuss it when it's returned. Through understanding, give understanding.

▪ YouTube link The Case for Christ:
www.youtube.com/watch?v=XqgQ9g2MV_8

More ideas at GreatWithGod.com

APPEAL TO HEAVEN: Using the **Ripple Intercession Index** prayer, focus on the Spirit of Understanding.

SUNDAY: FAMILY. Father, I ask You to give me a heart like Solomon, a wise and understanding heart. Teach me to discern with whom to share Your pearls of truth. Help my family to understand each other.

MONDAY: CHURCH. Jesus, You said, "Upon this rock I would build my church": the rock of a man's understanding that You are the Messiah. Cause my church to become active in fulfilling the Great Commission.

TUESDAY: COMMUNITY. I pray that You would give our schoolteachers and administrators a spirit of understanding. Give them all insight to know that You are the creator and designer of the universe and that You therefore understand how our bodies, minds and social relationships work best.

WEDNESDAY: CITY. Holy Spirit, grant a spirit of understanding to my mayor. Grant deep insight for the solving of complex problems and then help them implement wise plans that reflect Your perspective.

THURSDAY: STATE. Give us godly leaders. Let there be the passing of laws in my state that honor Your word and bring glory to Your name.

FRIDAY: NATION. I pray the prayer of John Knox, "Lord, give me Scotland or I die." Lord give me my nation (name out loud). Raise up evangelists who will understand the great needs of our times and preach relevant messages.

SATURDAY: WORLD. I pray that the world would be convinced of Your reality because of the love that Christians demonstrate toward one another. Lord, grant the family of faith around the world "hearing hearts."

Spirit of Counsel

THE IMAGE OF GOD: "For a child is born to us, a son is given to us. The government will rest on his shoulders. And he will be called: Wonderful Counselor, Mighty God, Everlasting Father, Prince of Peace" (Is. 9:6).

▪ "But I will send you the Advocate(counselor)—the Spirit of truth. He will come to you from the Father and will testify all about me" (Jn. 15:26).

▪ "O Sovereign Lord! You made the heavens and earth by your strong hand and powerful arm. Nothing is too hard for you! …You have all wisdom and do great and mighty miracles. You see the conduct of all people, and you give them what they deserve" (Jer. 32:17, 19).

— KEEP YOUR WORD —

THE COMMAND OF CHRIST: "You know our ancestors were told, 'Don't use the Lord's name to make a promise unless you are going to keep it.' But I tell you not to swear by anything when you make a promise! Heaven is God's throne, so don't swear by heaven. The earth is God's footstool, so don't swear by the earth. Jerusalem is the city of the great king, so don't swear by it. Don't swear by your own head. You cannot make one hair white or black. When you make a promise, say only 'Yes' or 'No.' Anything else comes from the devil" (Matt. 5:33-37 cev).

▪ "When you make a promise to God, don't delay in following through, for God takes no pleasure in fools. Keep all the promises you make to him. It is better to say nothing than to make a promise and not keep it" (Ecc. 5:4-5).

- "All praise to God, the Father of our Lord Jesus Christ. God is our merciful Father and the source of all comfort. He comforts us in all our troubles so that we can comfort others. When they are troubled, we will be able to give them the same comfort God has given us" (2 Cor. 1:3-4).
- "When you are arrested, don't worry about how to respond or what to say. God will give you the right words at the right time" (Matt. 10:19).

✓ —— LIVING IN ALIGNMENT WITH THE WONDERFUL COUNSELOR ——

☐ What are the characteristics of a wonderful counselor?
☐ Am I a trustworthy counselor?
☐ Do I keep my word even if it means an unexpected sacrifice to do so?
☐ Do I see my present trials and troubles as future platforms for comforting others?
☐ Do I know how to recognize the promptings of the Holy Spirit?
☐ Have I trained "my ear" to hear God's voice?
☐ What's the difference between swearing and making a vow to God?

FAITH IN ACTION: MAKE A VOW

- Consider making a short term vow to God. Use a vow as a catalyst to do a hard noble thing you won't do otherwise. Pray and then do it. Using a vow is asking for God to give His power to help you carry it out. But is also a serious promise to God that He will hold you accountable to fulfill. Read Ecclesiastes 5:4-5.

More ideas at GreatWithGod.com

APPEAL TO HEAVEN: Using the **Ripple Intercession** index prayer, focus on the Spirit of Counsel ministering to the least, last and lost.

SUNDAY: FAMILY. Spirit of Counsel, there are so many voices giving advice today. Help me to discern the truth. Come be my guide, teacher, and counselor. I pray for my parents to give wise counsel to each of their children.

MONDAY: CHURCH. Wonderful Counselor, I pray to You for the pastors of my church. I ask that You fill them with a spirit of counsel. As they study Your word, teach them how to make practical application in our culture.

TUESDAY: COMMUNITY. Wonderful Counselor, let there be the formation of Christian counseling clinics in my community. Raise up godly men and women who will serve our community as shepherding counselors.

WEDNESDAY: CITY. Heavenly Father, there are many sick who need a touch from the great physician. Heal their bodies and raise up chaplains to visit the sick in hospitals and minister to souls with a spirit of wise counsel.

THURSDAY: STATE. Dear God, whose very nature is freedom, raise up nurturing evangelistic teams who will go to prisons and share wise counsel. Send Your truth to set the captives free.

FRIDAY: NATION. Holy Spirit, raise up deacons in every church in my nation to provide practical assistance to widows. Endow each helper with a spirit of counsel.

SATURDAY: WORLD. Our Father, which art in heaven, You promised to be a father to the fatherless. Raise up care for orphans around the world. Provide funds and buildings, programs and ministries.

Spirit of Might

THE IMAGE OF GOD: "He has made the earth by His power, He has established the world by His wisdom, and has stretched out the heavens at His discretion. When He utters His voice, there is a multitude of water in the heavens: And He causes the vapors to ascend from the ends of the earth. He makes lightning for the rain, He brings the wind out of His treasuries" (Jer. 10:12-13).

▪ "The mighty God, even the Lord, hath spoken, and called the earth from the rising of the sun unto the going down thereof" (Ps. 50:1 KJV).

▪ "And Jesus came and spake unto them, saying, All power is given unto me in heaven and in earth" (Matt. 28:1).

— FEAR NOT —

THE COMMAND OF CHRIST: "Don't be afraid of those who want to kill your body; they cannot touch your soul. Fear only God, who can destroy both soul and body in hell" (MATT. 10:28).

▪ "A final word: Be strong in the Lord and in his mighty power. Put on all of God's armor so that you will be able to stand firm against all strategies of the devil…. Therefore, put on every piece of God's armor so you will be able to resist the enemy in the time of evil. Then after the battle you will still be standing firm" (EPH. 6:10-11, 13).

▪ "This is my command—be strong and courageous! Do not be afraid or discouraged. For the Lord your God is with you wherever you go" (JOSH. 1:9).

▪ "For God has not given us a spirit of fear and timidity, but of power, love, and self-discipline" (2 Tim. 1:7).

▪ "In that day it shall be said to Jerusalem: Do not fear; Zion let not your hands be weak. The Lord your God is in your midst, the Mighty One, will save; He will rejoice over you with gladness, He will quiet you with His love, He will rejoice over you with singing" (ZEPH. 3:16-17).

▪ "Then call on me when you are in trouble, and I will rescue you, and you will give me glory" (Ps. 50:15).

▪ "But the Lord is faithful; he will strengthen you and guard you from the evil one" (2 THES. 3:3).

✓── LIVING IN ALIGNMENT WITH THE SPIRIT OF POWER AND MIGHT ──

☐ What do I fear? Why?

☐ When I am in trouble is calling on God the first thing I do or the last thing I do?

☐ What does it mean that God is sovereign?

☐ Do I fully trust that Jesus defeated the devil through His death and resurrection?

☐ Do I put on the armor of God daily by readying my mind with God's truth?

☐ What does it mean when God doesn't deliver me from the trouble I'm in?

FAITH IN ACTION: INVITE A FRIEND TO CHURCH

▪ Invite and take a friend to church this Sunday. If they have an excuse, you have two options: try someone else or go for the reschedule. You're not done till someone comes.

More ideas at GreatWithGod.com

APPEAL TO HEAVEN: Use the **Ripple Intercession Index** prayer to focus on the raising up and releasing of the ministries of the Spirit (1 COR. 12) in power and might

SUNDAY: FAMILY. Spirit of might, fill me now with the grace I need to fulfill the ministry of helping the other members of my family. Raise me up to be an evangelist.

MONDAY: CHURCH. Lord Almighty, thank You for my church and pastors. I pray that You would protect and keep my home church (list it by name) and through my pastors display Your miraculous power to an unbelieving world.

TUESDAY: COMMUNITY. Holy Spirit raise up a ministry of healing in my neighborhood. Manifest Your power and miracle ministry to my neighbors.

WEDNESDAY: CITY. Holy Spirit raise up a prophetic ministry in my city. Raise prophets from within our midst to speak the truth in love.

THURSDAY: STATE. Lord, today, I pray for my state, that You would raise up ministries to care for orphans and widows. Raise up ministries to defend and feed the poor. Give the leaders of such ministries Your spirit of power and might.

FRIDAY: NATION. For my national leaders, I ask You to give them each a spirit of power and might. Hear their prayers and prove Yourself strong by delivering this nation from evil. (Pray for Your president and representatives by name.)

SATURDAY: WORLD. Today I pray for my apostolic church planting missionary friends (list any You know by name). Holy Spirit, infuse them with a spirit of courage, power and might. Cause them to be effective in their work for You and release a ministry of translating the gospel.

Spirit of Knowledge

THE IMAGE OF GOD: "And the Spirit of the Lord will rest on him— the Spirit of wisdom and understanding, the Spirit of counsel and might, the Spirit of knowledge and the fear of the Lord. He will delight in obeying the Lord. He will not judge by appearance nor make a decision based on hearsay" (Is. 11:2-3).

▪ "Then the Lord spoke to Moses saying, 'I have filled him (Bezalel) with the Spirit of God, in wisdom, in understanding, in knowledge, and in all manner of workmanship'" (Ex. 31:3).

— HONOR GOD'S LAW —

THE COMMAND OF CHRIST: "Don't misunderstand why I have come. I did not come to abolish the law of Moses or the writings of the prophets. No, I came to accomplish their purpose. I tell you the truth, until heaven and earth disappear, not even the smallest detail of God's law will disappear until its purpose is achieved" (MATT. 5:17-18).

▪ "You, through Your commandments, make me wiser than my enemies; For they are ever with me. I have more understanding than all my teachers, For Your testimonies are my meditation. I understand more than the ancients, Because I keep Your precepts" (Ps. 119:98-100).

▪ "Be careful to obey all the instructions Moses gave you. Do not deviate from them, turning either to the right or to the left. Then you will be careful in everything you do. Study this Book of Instruction continually. Meditate on it day and night so you will be sure to obey everything written in it. Only then will you prosper and succeed in all you do" (JOSH. 1:7-8).

- "Daniel answered and said: 'Blessed be the name of God forever and ever, for wisdom and might are His. And He changes the times and the seasons; He removes kings and raises up kings; He gives wisdom to the wise and knowledge to those who have understanding. He reveals deep and secret things; He knows what is in the darkness, and light dwells with Him'" (DAN. 2:20-22).

- "A spiritual gift is given to each of us so we can help each other. To one person the Spirit gives the ability to give wise advice; to another the same Spirit gives a message of special knowledge" (1 COR. 12:7-8).

✓ —— LIVING IN ALIGNMENT WITH THE SPIRIT OF KNOWLEDGE ——

☐ What does it mean to fear the Lord?
☐ What does it mean to meditate on God's word?
☐ What is the difference between wisdom, understanding and knowledge?
☐ How can I cultivate a relationship with the Holy Spirit?
☐ Can I identify the prompting from the Holy Spirit?

FAITH IN ACTION: GIVE A BIBLE

- You have so many ways to fulfill this assignment. Consider giving an electronic app version of the Bible. Consider giving a paper version of Bible, or perhaps an audio Bible. Or just give the New Testament or the Gospel of John. Last of all, please consider purchasing a Bible for someone in another country.

More ideas at GreatWithGod.com

Appeal to Heaven: Use the Ripple Intercession **Index** prayer to focus on the Spirit of Knowledge.

Sunday: Family. (Pray for Your family members by name) Omniscient Father, with You there is no darkness. Give me and my family members a spirit of knowledge of Jesus Christ. Today I ask that You grant a saving knowledge of Jesus Christ to each of my family members.

Monday: Church. I pray for the elders of my church. Thank You, Father, for the volunteer service of our leaders. Grant them each a spirit of knowledge that leads to unity.

Tuesday: Community. Think of the names of the neighbors You know and pray for them by name. Ask God to grant them a saving knowledge of Jesus Christ.

Wednesday: City. Cause the citizens of my city to have hearts of flesh. Make them ready to hear the truth. And send forth Your pastors to boldly proclaim the message of truth.

Thursday: State. I ask that You would raise up institutions and ministries to publish a knowledge of God in every creative way. Raise up Bible apps and online teaching opportunities.

Friday: Nation. God, provide resources for our Christian radio and TV stations to continue to broadcast the gospel.

Saturday: World. Spirit of knowledge, grant spiritual insight to those who are serving as missionaries. I ask You to raise up ministries to publish, translate and distribute written Bibles, oral Bibles, and audio Bible lessons in every language.

Spirit of the Fear
OF THE LORD

THE IMAGE OF GOD: "And the Spirit of the LORD will rest on him—the Spirit of wisdom and understanding, the Spirit of counsel and might, the Spirit of knowledge and the fear of the LORD" (Is. 11:2).

- "I saw the dead, both great and small, standing before God's throne. And the books were opened, including the Book of Life. And the dead were judged according to what they had done, as recorded in the books" (REV. 20:12).
- "The LORD is watching everywhere, keeping his eye on both the evil and the good" (PROV. 15:3).
- "You know when I sit down or stand up. You know my thoughts even when I'm far away. You see me when I travel and when I rest at home. You know everything I do. You know what I am going to say even before I say it, Lord. You go before me and follow me. I can never escape from your Spirit! I can never get away from your presence! If I go up to heaven, you are there; if I go down to the grave, you are there" (Ps. 139:2-8).

— REPENT —

THE COMMAND OF CHRIST: "From then on Jesus began to preach, 'Repent of your sins and turn to God, for the Kingdom of Heaven is near'"(MATT. 4:17).

- "For the LORD disciplines those he loves, and he punishes each one he accepts as his child" (HEB. 12:6).
- "I correct and discipline everyone I love. So be diligent and turn from your indifference" (REV. 3:19).
- "For we must all stand before Christ to be judged. We will each receive whatever we deserve for the good or evil we have done in this earthly body" (2 COR. 5:10).

- "Better to have little, with fear for the LORD, than to have great treasure and inner turmoil" (PROV. 15:16).
- "These are the commands, decrees, and regulations that the LORD your God commanded me to teach you. You must obey them in the land you are about to enter and occupy, and you and your children and grandchildren must fear the LORD your God as long as you live. If you obey all his decrees and commands, you will enjoy a long life" (DEUT. 6:1-2).
- "But put on the Lord Jesus Christ, and make no provision for the flesh, to fulfill its lusts" (ROM.13:14).

✓ — LIVING IN ALIGNMENT WITH THE FEAR OF THE LORD —

- ☐ On a scale of 1-10, how aware am I that God is continuously evaluating everything I think, say and do?
- ☐ Does having an awareness that God will one day judge all my actions impact my behavior?
- ☐ How do I demonstrate true repentance?
- ☐ Can I give an example from my life of how the Lord's discipline equaled as an expression of His love?
- ☐ What if I ignore the Lord's discipline?
- ☐ What can I do to cultivate the fear of the Lord in my life?
- ☐ Am I convinced that faith is greater than riches?

FAITH IN ACTION: DISCARD DISTRACTIONS

- The idea is simply to rid your life of anything that the Holy Spirit is convicting you of that hinders your relationship to Him. Is there any competing affection or activity in your life? If so, re-prioritize or discard it.

More ideas at GreatWithGod.com

APPEAL TO HEAVEN: Use the **Ripple Intercession Index** prayer while focusing on the Spirit of the Fear of the Lord.

SUNDAY: FAMILY. Lord God Almighty, have mercy upon me according to the multitude of Your tender mercies. Blot out my parents' transgressions. Cleanse my family by the blood of the lamb.

MONDAY: CHURCH. I pray for my pastors that You would increase their respect for You that they may grow in wisdom.

TUESDAY: COMMUNITY. I specifically pray for the salvation of our school teachers and medical doctors. Pray for Your teachers and Your family doctor by name. Ask God to grant them the gift of repentance unto salvation.

WEDNESDAY: CITY: God, whose very nature is order, thank You for the police officers who serve to keep order in my city. Defend those who defend us. Teach all who live in my city to honor government officials as Your ministers for peace.

THURSDAY: STATE. God Almighty, You are the one true perfect judge. I praise You for You alone are worthy to stand as judge of all people. I pray for the judges in my state. Cause them to hate bribes and to defend the poor.

FRIDAY: NATION. Lord Jesus, You are ruler over all. So I pray for those who serve in the military. Bless each soldier and keep them and defend them with Your heavenly grace.

SATURDAY: WORLD. God of angel armies, come and reign over the nations of the world. Disable the power of Satan so that a knowledge and fear of the Lord can cover the earth unhindered.

44 *the Holy Spirit is Holy*

THE IMAGE OF GOD: "Give the following instructions to the entire community of Israel. You must be holy because I, the LORD your God, am holy" (LEV. 19:2).

■ "The first of these living beings was like a lion; the second was like an ox; the third had a human face; and the fourth was like an eagle in flight. Each of these living beings had six wings, and their wings were covered all over with eyes, inside and out. Day after day and night after night they keep on saying, 'Holy, holy, holy is the Lord God, the Almighty—the one who always was, who is, and who is still to come'" (Rev. 4:7-8).

■ "Pray like this: Our Father in heaven, may your name be kept holy" (MATT. 6:9).

— CHOOSE THE NARROW WAY —

THE COMMAND OF CHRIST: "You can enter God's Kingdom only through the narrow gate. The highway to hell is broad, and its gate is wide for the many who choose that way. But the gateway to life is very narrow and the road is difficult, and only a few ever find it" (MATT. 7:13-14).

■ "Run from sexual sin! No other sin so clearly affects the body as this one does. For sexual immorality is a sin against your own body. Don't you realize that your body is the temple of the Holy Spirit, who lives in you and was given to you by God? You do not belong to yourself, for God bought you with a high price. So you must honor God with your body" (1 COR. 6:18-20).

▪ "They do not belong to this world any more than I do. Make them holy by your truth; teach them your word, which is truth. Just as you sent Me into the world, I am sending them into the world. And I give Myself as a holy sacrifice for them so they can be made holy by Your truth" (Jn. 17:16-19).

▪ "And you will be My kingdom of priests, My holy nation" (Ex. 19:6).

▪ "I have hidden your word in my heart, that I might not sin against you" (Ps. 119:11).

✓   — LIVING IN ALIGNMENT WITH THE HOLY SPIRIT —

☐ In what way am I friends with the world that I should not be?

☐ What does it mean to be holy?

☐ What roles does truth play in my holiness?

☐ What must I do to guard my sexual purity?

☐ What does it mean that my body belongs to God?

☐ Do I defend God's reputation?

☐ How does my holiness affect my ability to witness?

FAITH IN ACTION: DANIEL FAST

▪ Limited fast for five consecutive days. Read Daniel Chapter 10. Restrict your diet. No meat, appetizers, desserts, candy, or bread (donuts). Water will be your only beverage for this fast. Delight in God with reading, singing and service. Fast for a spiritual breakthrough. Ask God, "What manifestation of Your kingdom would You like to see on earth?"

More ideas at GreatWithGod.com

APPEAL TO HEAVEN: Use the **Ripple Intercession Index** prayer while focusing on the Spirit of Holiness.

SUNDAY: FAMILY. Holy Spirit, I pray for my aunts, uncles and cousins. Make them holy by Your truth (call their personal names out in prayer). Make me a channel of Your love to my extended family. Prepare their hearts to receive truth and grant me courage to share it with them.

MONDAY: CHURCH. Holy Spirit, please do whatever is necessary to make Your church holy. Raise up a generation of pastors who will pursue and preach holiness.

TUESDAY: COMMUNITY. Holy Spirit, I recognize that You give each believer a spiritual gift. I pray for those You have gifted as teachers.. Guide them into all truth.

WEDNESDAY: CITY. Holy Spirit, send holy prophets to speak truth to Your church. Send us courageous prophets to pr claim truth in the church and to the city.

THURSDAY: STATE. Holy Spirit, raise up a new generation of worship leaders. Let teams of skillful musician compose new songs to lead Your people in holy worship.

FRIDAY: NATION. Lord of the harvest, I thank You for the evangelists You have given to this generation. Grant them favor so that my entire nation may hear of the saving knowledge of Christ.

SATURDAY: WORLD. Lord of the harvest, raise up missionaries to go to every tribe that is yet to hear the gospel. Jehovah Jireh, provide the funds necessary to support Your missionaries.

God is the Disciple

Beatitudes

Use the Body Position Alignment Index

Your Goal: Pray through the Body Position Index pray each day. Then pray for 5 minutes concerning the index theme assigned each day. Use the prayer guide at the end of each chapter to help you get started.

On Saturday, complete your meditation for the week by praying completely through the Prayer Wheel Index in 35 minutes

The source and inspiration for the all the body positions and much of their accompanying meaning comes from the Anger Resolution Seminar published by the Institute a Basic Life Principles as published in their workbook.

THE BODY POSITION INDEX PRAYER

JESUS, hear my prayer as I choose to align my body in harmony with the attitude of my praying. It is awesome to come into Your presence. I am not worthy, I am not qualified (**on my face: in humility**). On my own I am not righteous; I have only that righteousness which You have given me through faith in the name and the blood of Jesus Christ. I am sorry for my sinful (**kneeling: in grief**) ways and turn from them now. I want Your will, not mine (**bowing: in meekness**), for my life. I am hungry for You (**standing: in righteousness**). Have mercy upon me (**sitting: mercifully**) according to Your loving kindness. Purify my motives (**looking up: pure in heart**) and sign me up to be Your peacemaker (**my arm stretched forth: peacemaker**) even in the face of possible persecution (**leaping for joy: persecuted**). Amen.

Inspiration for the body alignment index from Bill Gothard, the Prayer Positions for the Body Aligned with the 8 Beatitudes.[10]

Humility

THE IMAGE OF GOD: "You must have the same attitude that Christ Jesus had. Though he was God, he did not think of equality with God as something to cling to. Instead, he gave up his divine privileges; he took the humble position of a slave and was born as a human being. When he appeared in human form, he humbled himself in obedience to God and died a criminal's death on a cross. Therefore, God elevated him to the place of highest honor and gave him the name above all other names, that at the name of Jesus every knee should bow, in heaven and on earth and under the earth, and every tongue declare that Jesus Christ is Lord, to the glory of God the Father" (PHIL. 2:5-11).

▪ "Take my yoke upon you and learn from me, for I am gentle and humble in heart, and you will find rest for your souls" (MATT. 11:29).

▪ "And whoever wants to be first must be your slave—just as the Son of Man did not come to be served, but to serve, and to give his life as a ransom for many" (MATT. 20:27-28).

— BE BORN AGAIN —

THE COMMAND OF CHRIST: "Jesus replied, 'I assure you, no one can enter the Kingdom of God without being born of water and the Spirit. Humans can reproduce only human life, but the Holy Spirit gives birth to spiritual life. So don't be surprised when I say, You must be born again'" (JN. 3:5-7, 19).

▪ "If you declare with your mouth, 'Jesus is Lord,' and believe in your heart that God raised him from the dead, you will be saved" (ROM. 10:9).

▪ "God blesses those who are poor in spirit and realize their need for Him, for the Kingdom of Heaven is theirs" (MATT. 5:3).

▪ "There is one that makes himself rich, yet has nothing: And one who makes himself poor, yet great riches. The ransom of a man's life is his riches, But the poor does not hear rebuke" (PROV. 13:7-8).

▪ "For you know the grace of our Lord Jesus Christ, that though He was rich, yet for your sakes He became poor, that you through His poverty might become rich" (2 COR. 8:9).

✓ ── LIVING IN ALIGNMENT WITH THE ATTITUDE OF HUMILITY ──

☐ What are the evidences of true humility?

☐ Have my earthly treasures become a hindrance to my allegiance to God?

☐ Do I consider others better than myself?

☐ Do I have any problem submitting to authority?

☐ How would I know if I am I overly impressed with position, prestige, or possessions?

☐ What do I have that I have not been given?

☐ Have I ever shared my faith with someone else?

☐ How can I know I've been born again?

FAITH IN ACTION: GIVE THE GOSPEL

▪ Give a gospel pamphlet. First read it yourself, then decide to whom you might give it. Look at your Top 5 list. If you've been praying for this person, trust God to do the rest.

▪ Online tools to share your faith on website

More ideas at GreatWithGod.com

APPEAL TO HEAVEN: Prayer Position For the Humble in Spirit: on our faces before God, which is to lay on the ground face down before God, expressing humility.

SUNDAY: PRAYING ON MY FACE expressing my total unworthiness. I am not qualified. I am not capable. I am weak and I am trusting You, God, to give me Your strength and wisdom.

MONDAY: PRAYING ON MY FACE expressing my need for mercy: I acknowledge that I was wrong when I_____. Please forgive me. I need Your mercy.

TUESDAY: PRAYING ON MY FACE in desperation: Dear God, I recognize Your hand in allowing personal calamity in my life that I might turn to You in my moment of need. I call upon You in this day of trouble. Come deliver me. My hope is in You.

WEDNESDAY: PRAYING ON MY FACE acknowledging that I am not Lord but He is Lord: I am laying down my agenda and choosing to live for Your agenda.

THURSDAY: STATE: PRAYING ON MY FACE humbly acknowledging that I don't have the power to change myself, but Lord, You can change me. Conform me to the image of Your Son.

FRIDAY: PRAYING ON MY FACE surrendering to Your will. Realizing that the thing You want done is usually not the thing I want to do. Your will, not mine.

SATURDAY: PRAYING ON MY FACE acknowledging that all the success in my life is from God and not because of anything I have done.

Mourn/Compassion

THE IMAGE OF GOD: "All praise to God, the Father of our Lord Jesus Christ. God is our merciful Father and the source of all comfort. He comforts us in all our troubles so that we can comfort others. When they are troubled, we will be able to give them the same comfort God has given us. For the more we suffer for Christ, the more God will shower us with his comfort through Christ. Even when we are weighed down with troubles, it is for your comfort and salvation! For when we ourselves are comforted, we will certainly comfort you. Then you can patiently endure the same things we suffer" (2 COR. 1:3-6).

- "The Spirit of the Sovereign LORD is upon me, for the LORD has anointed me to bring good news to the poor. He has sent me to comfort the brokenhearted and to proclaim that captives will be released and prisoners will be freed. He has sent me to tell those who mourn that the time of the LORD's favor has come" (Is. 61:1-2).

— BEWARE OF COVETOUSNESS —

THE COMMAND OF CHRIST: "Then he said, 'Beware! Guard against every kind of greed. Life is not measured by how much you own'" (LUKE 12:15).

- "You must not covet your neighbor's house. You must not covet your neighbor's wife, male or female servant, ox or donkey, or anything else that belongs to your neighbor" (Ex. 20:17).

- "Don't love money; be satisfied with what you have. For God has said, 'I will never fail you. I will never abandon you'" (HEB. 13:5).

▪ "God blesses those who mourn, for they will be comforted" (MATT. 5:4).

▪ "To all who mourn in Israel, he will give a crown of beauty for ashes, a joyous blessing instead of mourning, festive praise instead of despair. In their righteousness, they will be like great oaks that the LORD has planted for his own glory" (Is. 61:3).

✓ —— LIVING IN ALIGNMENT WITH THE ATTITUDE OF COMPASSION ——

☐ Am I guilty of loving things and using people? What adjustment will be needed to change this?

☐ Am I able to overcome my sorrow and allow God to comfort me?

☐ In what ways does God comfort His people?

☐ Have the cares of this world contributed to my seasons of mourning?

☐ Have I experienced God transforming my mourning into joy?

☐ How does my heart get broken?

☐ Am I a source of comfort to the hurting lives around me?

FAITH IN ACTION: 222 PAY IT FORWARD

▪ Do a kind deed for someone. Here's the caveat: If they say thank you, then reply, "You're welcome. Would you consider paying it forward?" If they ask what you mean, suggest that they pay kindness forward to another person before the day is over. Multiply kindness.

▪ If you choose to give a gift, include a note explaining the program and ask them to pay it forward.

More ideas at GreatWithGod.com

APPEAL TO HEAVEN: Prayer Position For Those Who Have Compassion and Grieve Over Sin: kneeling before God.

SUNDAY: PRAYING ON MY KNEES I acknowledge that You are Lord of my life. I bow before You as my king. Every knee will bow and every tongue shall confess that Jesus Christ is Lord.

MONDAY: PRAYING ON MY KNEES I make my earnest appeal to You. You are Lord God almighty. Nothing is impossible with You. I am on my knees asking You to hear and answer this prayer request.

TUESDAY: PRAYING ON MY KNEES adding fervency to my prayers. Lord, I am sincere in my repentance. Give me the power today to live a holy life.

WEDNESDAY: PRAYING ON MY KNEES acknowledging I can do all things through Christ who strengthens me. I ask for the power of Christ and, more importantly, I am laying down my agenda and choosing to live for Your agenda.

THURSDAY: STATE: PRAYING ON MY KNEES acknowledging that I am lacking compassion, but You are a God whose very essence is compassion. Change my heart to conform to Your heart. Give me a heart of compassion.

FRIDAY: PRAYING ON MY KNEES realizing that there is a propensity in my life to love things and use people. Lord, You want just the opposite. Help me see people the way You see people.

SATURDAY: PRAYING ON MY KNEES acknowledging that all the success in my life is because of God. All that I am is because You have made me so.

Meek

THE IMAGE OF GOD: "Let this mind be in you, which was also in Christ Jesus: Who, being in the form of God, thought it not robbery to be equal with God: But made himself of no reputation, and took upon him the form of a servant, and was made in the likeness of men" (PHIL. 2:5-7 KJV).

▪ "But let it be the hidden man of the heart, in that which is not corruptible, even the ornament of a meek and quiet spirit, which is in the sight of God of great price" (1 PET. 3:4, KJV).

▪ "Going a little farther, he fell with his face to the ground and prayed, 'My Father, if it is possible, may this cup be taken from me. Yet not as I will, but as you will'" (Matt. 26:39).

▪ "By myself I can do nothing; I judge only as I hear, and my judgment is just, for I seek not to please myself but him who sent me" (JN. 5:30).

— TAKE MY YOKE —

THE COMMAND OF CHRIST: "Then Jesus said, 'Come to me, all of you who are weary and carry heavy burdens, and I will give you rest. Take my yoke upon you. Let me teach you, because I am humble and gentle at heart, and you will find rest for your souls. For my yoke is easy to bear, and the burden I give you is light'" (MATT. 11:28-30).

▪ "Give all your worries and cares to God, for he cares about you" (1 PET. 5:7).

▪ "Don't worry about anything; instead, pray about everything. Tell God what you need, and thank him for all he has done" (PHIL. 4:6).

- "Give your burdens to the LORD, and he will take care of you. He will not permit the godly to slip and fall" (Ps. 55:22).
- "The meek will he guide in judgment: and the meek will he teach his way" (Ps. 25:9 KJV).
- "Blessed are the meek for they shall inherit the earth" (MATT. 5:5 KJV).

✓ —— LIVING IN ALIGNMENT WITH THE ATTITUDE OF MEEKNESS ——

☐ What is the meaning of the word meek?
☐ Have I surrendered my ambitions to the Lord?
☐ Am I only saying that I follow God or am I doing it?
☐ Am I willing to follow Jesus even if it means suffering for Him?
☐ How is it that meekness is a prerequisite for guidance?
☐ Am I experiencing the light load of Christ or the heavy load of carrying my own burdens?
☐ Is my heart anxious about anything?
☐ What must I do to enter into the Lord's rest for me?
☐ How can I cultivate meekness?
☐ How did Christ demonstrate meekness?

FAITH IN ACTION: WORKPLACE JERICHO PRAYER WALK

- Pray as you walk around the outside perimeter of your office. Pray as you intentionally walk down the hallways. Use the different work areas as a type of prayer index (such as the break room, copy room, conference room). And pray at the entrance of your place of work. Ask God to grant eternal life to all who enter.

More ideas at GreatWithGod.com

Appeal to Heaven: Prayer Position for Meekness: bowing ourselves before the Lord.

Sunday: I Bow Myself Before You, Lord, as a sign of my reverence. Heavenly Father, I respect You and Your right to lead Your family. You are worthy of my respect because You have_____ .

Monday: I Bow Myself Before You, Lord, as a sign of my worship. I acknowledge that all things come from Your hand. I bow in gratitude and thank You for_____. I acknowledge this was gift from You.

Tuesday: I Bow Myself Before You, Lord, as an act of praise. I praise You for You are both good and great. You have done all things well. You alone are worthy of my praise.

Wednesday: I Bow Myself Before You, Lord, acknowledging that I am not Lord but You are Lord. I can do all things through Christ who strengthens me. Let the power of Christ be manifested in my life.

Thursday: I Bow Myself Before You, Lord, acknowledging that I don't have the power to change things, but You do. Lord God, nothing is impossible with You. I surrender what I want; please change the desires of my heart so that they will match the desires of Your heart.

Friday: I Bow Myself Before You, Lord, surrendering my own will to Your will. I realizing that the thing You want done is usually not the thing I want done. I believe I am in You and You are in me. Thy will be done, not mine.

Saturday: I Bow Myself Before You, Lord. You are the only source of my successes. List Your (His) successes in Your life. Give Him thanks and give Him praise.

Hunger and Thirst
FOR RIGHTEOUSNESS

THE IMAGE OF GOD: "Righteousness and justice are the foundation of your throne; love and faithfulness go before you" (Ps. 89:14).

▪ "This is what the LORD says: 'Don't let the wise boast in their wisdom, or the powerful boast in their power, or the rich boast in their riches. But those who wish to boast should boast in this alone: that they truly know me and understand that I am the LORD who demonstrates unfailing love and who brings justice and righteousness to the earth, and that I delight in these things. I, the LORD, have spoken!'" (JER. 9:23-24).

▪ "How can a young person stay pure? By obeying your word" (Ps. 119:9).

—– DO NOT COMMIT ADULTERY —–

THE COMMAND OF CHRIST: "You have heard the commandment that says, 'You must not commit adultery.' But I say, anyone who even looks at a woman with lust has already committed adultery with her in his heart. So if your eye—even your good eye—causes you to lust, gouge it out and throw it away. It is better for you to lose one part of your body than for your whole body to be thrown into hell" (MATT. 5:27-29).

▪ "For everything in the world—the lust of the flesh, the lust of the eyes, and the pride of life—comes not from the Father but from the world" (1 JN. 2:16).

▪ "Run from anything that stimulates youthful lusts. Instead, pursue righteous living, faithfulness, love, and peace. Enjoy the companionship of those who call on the Lord with pure hearts" (2 TIM. 2:22).

- "Blessed are those who hunger and thirst for righteousness for they shall be satisfied" (MATT. 5).
- "They shall neither hunger nor thirst, neither heat nor sun shall strike them; for He who has mercy on them will lead them, even the springs of water He will guide them" (Is. 49:10).
- "Take delight in the LORD, and he will give you your heart's desires" (Ps. 37:4).
- "You will seek me and find me when you seek me with all your heart" (JER. 29:13 NIV).

✓ —— LIVING IN ALIGNMENT BY HUNGERING FOR RIGHTEOUSNESS ——

☐ Is there evidence that my heart is consumed with the lust of the flesh and the pride of life?
☐ What evidence is there that my heart is persuing God?
☐ What's the difference between being content in God and being hungry for more of God?
☐ What can I do to cultivate a pure heart that desires God as highest priority?
☐ How can I deliver myself from the lust of the flesh?
☐ What plan can be made to protect my sexual purity?

FAITH IN ACTION: WAR ON LUST

- Agree with God that it's not in alignment with His righteous design. Ask for His help. Get rid of anything that contributes to your failure to overcome lust. Get an accountability partner or mentor.

More ideas at GreatWithGod.com

APPEAL TO HEAVEN: **Prayer Position for Righteousness:** standing before the Lord.

SUNDAY: **I STAND BEFORE YOU, LORD,** with confidence because Christ's righteousness is now mine through His shed blood which cleanses me from sin.

MONDAY: **I STAND BEFORE YOU, LORD,** today prepared for battle, for it is written, "We wrestle not against flesh and blood, but against spiritual powers of evil, therefore take up the full armor of God, that You may be able to withstand in the evil day, and having done all to stand. Stand therefore." Lord, today I stand. I will not retreat.

TUESDAY: **I STAND, LORD,** ready to serve. You have exalted me for such a time as this to serve those people whom You have brought into my life.

WEDNESDAY: **I STAND, LORD,** acknowledging that I am not righteous but that You are completely righteous. I am asking for the power of Christ be manifest in my life today that I may be a vessel of righteousness.

THURSDAY: **I STAND, LORD,** acknowledging that I don't have the power to change things, but You do. Lord Your very essence is righteousness, and since I am in You and You are in me, please change the desires of my heart so that they match the desires of Your heart.

FRIDAY: **I STAND BEFORE YOU, LORD,** realizing that the thing You want done is usually not the thing I want to do. I acknowledge that I don't want to _____ but I sense that You want me to_____. I surrender to Your will.

SATURDAY: **I STAND, LORD,** ready to serve. Here I am; send me to do Your work.

Merciful

The Image of God: "Then the Lord came down in a cloud and stood there with him; and he called out his own name, Yahweh. The Lord passed in front of Moses, calling out, 'Yahweh! The Lord! The God of compassion and mercy! I am slow to anger and filled with unfailing love and faithfulness'" (Ex. 34:5-6).

▪ "Now therefore, says the Lord, turn to Me with all your heart, with fasting, with weeping, and with mourning. So rend your heart, and not your garments; return to the Lord your God, for He is gracious and merciful, slow to anger, and of great kindness; and He relents from doing harm" (Joel 2:12-13).

▪ "Praise be to the God and Father of our Lord Jesus Christ, the Father of compassion and the God of all comfort" (2 Cor. 1:3).

— LOVE YOUR NEIGHBORS —

The Command of Christ: "A second is equally important: 'Love your neighbor as yourself.' The entire law and all the demands of the prophets are based on these two commandments" (Matt. 22:39-40).

▪ "'Now which of these three would you say was a neighbor to the man who was attacked by bandits?' Jesus asked. The man replied, 'The one who showed him mercy.' Then Jesus said, 'Yes, now go and do the same'" (Luke 10:36-37).

▪ "Never pay back evil with more evil. Do things in such a way that everyone can see you are honorable. Do all that you can to live in peace with everyone" (Rom. 12:17-18).

▪ "If you really keep the royal law found in Scripture, 'Love your neighbor as yourself,' you are doing right" (Jam. 2:8-9).

GOD'S PROMISES: TO SHOW MERCY TO THOSE
WHO SHOW MERCY TO OTHERS

- "Blessed are the merciful for they shall obtain mercy" (MATT. 5:7).
- "Do not judge others, and you will not be judged. For you will be treated as you treat others. The standard you use in judging is the standard by which you will be judged" (MATT. 7:1-2).
- "There will be no mercy for those who have shown no mercy to others. But if you have been merciful, God will be merciful when he judges you" (JAM. 2:13).

✓ — **LIVING IN ALIGNMENT WITH THE MERCY OF GOD** —

☐ Have I shown as much mercy to others as I have received from God?

☐ Am I slow to become angry?

☐ Do I seek vengeance?

☐ How can I cultivate an attitude of mercy?

☐ When did someone show me mercy I did not deserve?

☐ What is a good definition of mercy?

☐ What do I want others to do for me? Figure this out and ask yourself, "How can I do that for others?"

☐ To whom will I show mercy today?

FAITH IN ACTION: NEIGHBORHOOD JERICHO PRAYER WALK

- Register at **www.blesseveryhome.com**. This powerful tool will enable you to pray for your hundred nearest neighbors by name and address. Ask God to bring His kingdom rule to all who live in your community. Pray for your neighbors by name Ask God to bless your neighbors with a revelation of Jesus Christ.

More ideas at GreatWithGod.com

APPEAL TO HEAVEN: **Prayer Position for the Merciful:** sitting before the Lord.

SUNDAY: **I SIT BEFORE YOU, LORD,** in recognition that You are in the place of final authority. All power resides in You. What You command is done. Hear my cause. Have mercy upon me.

MONDAY: **I SIT BEFORE YOU, LORD,** in recognition that You are the judge of all people. You are worthy to judge for You alone know all things. Have mercy upon my family.

TUESDAY: **I SIT, LORD,** acknowledging the great mystery that You declare that I am seated together with You at the right hand of the Father. Lord, You are greatly to be praised.

WEDNESDAY: **I SIT BEFORE YOU, LORD,** whose very nature is mercy. I can do all things through Christ who strengthens me. I am asking for the power of Christ to be manifested in my life today to display Your great mercy. Make me a vessel of mercy.

THURSDAY: **I SIT, LORD,** acknowledging that You are the ultimate Judge. I don't have the power to pardon and forgive sins, but You do. Lord God, nothing is impossible with You. I desire to be made into a vessel of Your mercy.

FRIDAY: **I SIT BEFORE YOU, LORD,** acknowledging that I don't want to grant mercy but I sense that You want me to show mercy to_____. I pray this way in a simple recognition that I am in You and You are in me.

SATURDAY: **I SIT BEFORE YOU, LORD,** acknowledging that all the successes in my life were because I was in You and You were in me.

Pure in Heart

THE IMAGE OF GOD: "'For I know the plans I have for you,' says the LORD. 'They are plans for good and not for disaster, to give you a future and a hope'"(JER. 29:11).

▪ "Looking for the…Savior Jesus Christ, who gave Himself for us, that He might redeem us from every lawless deed and purify for Himself His own special people, zealous for good works" (TITUS 2:13-14 KJV).

▪ "But the Lord said to Samuel, 'Don't judge by his appearance or height, for I have rejected him. The Lord doesn't see things the way you see them. People judge by outward appearance, but the Lord looks at the heart'" (1 SAM. 16:7).

▪ "The eyes of the LORD search the whole earth in order to strengthen those whose hearts are fully committed to him…" (2 CHRON. 16:9).

— BEWARE OF LEAVEN —

THE COMMAND OF CHRIST: "'Watch out!' Jesus warned them. 'Beware of the yeast of the Pharisees and Sadducees'"(MATT. 16:6).

▪ "Therefore submit to God, Resist the devil and he will flee from you. Draw near to God and He will draw near to you. Cleanse your hands, you sinners; and purify your hearts, you double-minded" (JAS. 4:7-8).

▪ "Now the purpose of the commandment is love from a pure heart, from a good conscience, and from sincere faith" (1 TIM. 1:5).

▪ "Don't let anyone capture you with empty philosophies and high-sounding nonsense that come from human thinking and from the spiritual powers of this world, rather than from Christ" (COL. 2:8).

▪ "God blesses those whose hearts are pure, for they will see God" (MATT. 5:8).

▪ "Guard your heart above all else, for it determines the course of your life" (PROV. 4:23).

▪ "If you keep yourself pure, you will be a special utensil for honorable use. Your life will be clean, ready for the Master to use you for every good work" (2 TIM. 2:21).

▪ "Come close to God, and God will come close to you. Wash your hands, you sinners; purify your hearts, for your loyalty is divided between God and the world" (JAM. 4:8).

✓ — LIVING IN ALIGNMENT WITH THE PURITY OF GOD —

☐ Does God purify me or do I purify myself?
☐ What practical steps can I take to purify my heart?
☐ What is the Holy Spirit convicting me is a bad influence that I must separate myself from?
☐ What are competing affections in my heart?
☐ What can I do today to draw near to God?
☐ What can I do today to resist temptation?
☐ In what ways do we reveal what's in our hearts?
☐ How can I guard my heart with all diligence, recognizing that my eyes and ears are the gates shaping my desires?

FAITH IN ACTION: WEAR A CROSS NECKLACE

▪ Wear a disciple's cross. When you put it on, say this prayer, "Lord, I give my life and my future to You. I wear this as reminder that I am belong to Christ and now He lives in me and I live in Him."

More ideas at GreatWithGod.com

APPEAL TO HEAVEN: Prayer Position For the Pure in Heart: looking up to heaven.

SUNDAY: I LOOK UP TO HEAVEN because You have given me a clean heart. You have made it possible for me to enjoy intimate fellowship with You. Oh Lord, I'm not perfect but I am completely forgiven. Thank You for saving me.

MONDAY: I LOOK UP and declare, I desire a clean heart. Give Your servant a heart that desires purity in all things.

TUESDAY: I LOOK UP TO HEAVEN with a desire to live in harmony with Your holy standards. Lord, give me wisdom and power to pursue a life of virtue and deliver me from evil.

WEDNESDAY: I LOOK UP acknowledging that I am not pure in heart but that You are, oh Lord. I ask for the power of Christ be manifest in my life today. Make me a vessel pure in heart. I do this in a simple recognition that I am in You and You are in me. Use me as a tool to help others become holy.

THURSDAY: I LOOK UP acknowledging that I am not pure in heart but that You are, oh Lord. I ask for the power of Christ be manifest in my life today. Make me a vessel pure in heart. Live and teach through me so I can help others become holy.

FRIDAY: I LOOK UP TO HEAVEN and surrender my own will to Your will. I want what You want, therefore, I want purity for myself. Be Lord of my life. You make the final decisions of my life.

SATURDAY: I LOOK UP TO HEAVEN asking for a pure heart. Make me a useful vessel for every good work of Yours.

Peacemakers

THE IMAGE OF GOD: "For to us a child is born, to us a son is given, and the government will be on his shoulders. And he will be called Wonderful Counselor, Mighty God, Everlasting Father, Prince of Peace" (Is. 9:6).

- "For He Himself is Our peace, who has made both One, and has broken down the middle wall of separation, having abolished in His flesh the enmity, that is, the law of commandments contained in ordinances, so as to create in Himself One new man from the two, thus making peace" (EPH. 2:14-15).

- "We are therefore Christ's ambassadors, as though God were making his appeal through us. We implore you on Christ's behalf: Be reconciled to God" (2 COR. 5:20).

— GO TO OFFENDERS —

THE COMMAND OF CHRIST: "If another believer sins against you, go privately and point out the offense. If the other person listens and confesses it, you have won that person back. But if you are unsuccessful, take one or two others with you and go back again, so that everything you say may be confirmed by two or three witnesses. If the person still refuses to listen, take your case to the church. Then if he or she won't accept the church's decision, treat that person as a pagan or a corrupt tax collector" (MATT. 18:15-17).

- "Dear brothers and sisters, if another believer is overcome by some sin, you who are godly should gently and humbly help that person back onto the right path. And be careful not to fall into the same temptation yourself" (GAL. 6:1).

- "Blessed are the peacemakers for they shall be called the children of God" (MATT. 5:8 KJV).
- "I am leaving you with a gift—peace of mind and heart. And the peace I give is a gift the world cannot give. So don't be troubled or afraid" (JN. 4:27).
- "Whenever you enter someone's home, first say, 'May God's peace be on this house'" (LUKE 10:5).

✓ — **LIVING IN ALIGNMENT WITH GOD'S DESIRE FOR PEACE** —

☐ What must I do to experience the peace of God?
☐ What does it mean to me that Jesus is a peacemaker?
☐ Contrast gossip and accusing as opposed to peacemaking.
☐ How is the peace of God different from the peace of the world?
☐ How can I experience peace in the midst of one of life's various storms?
☐ To whom will I be a peace maker today?
☐ Have I asked God to show me the beams that are in my own eye? What did He reveal to me?
☐ When I see faults in others do I use it to examine my own life?
☐ Where do I need to be a peacemaker? How?

FAITH IN ACTION: BLESS YOUR BOSS

- Bless your leader/boss/teacher this week. Put it in writing. Give your boss a handwritten thank you note/ card. Tell them that you pray for them and that God uses them to provide for you. Gifts may also be given.

More ideas at GreatWithGod.com

APPEAL TO HEAVEN: Prayer Position For the Peacemaker: stretching forth the arm.

SUNDAY: I STRETCH FORTH MY ARM in faith, believing that the things You have spoken to me will indeed come to pass. I stretch forth my arm and say let there be_____. (list the godly things You sense the Lord wants to accomplish through You and Your partners).

MONDAY: I STRETCH FORTH MY ARM, believing that You want to demonstrate Your power through my life. Make me a channel of Your power, love and self-control.

TUESDAY: I STRETCH FORTH MY ARM to speak forth Your blessings upon others. Lord God, grant Your power and desire to do Your will to my friends (list names). Turn their hearts toward You and deliver them from bondage to sin, the world and the devil.

WEDNESDAY: I STRETCH FORTH MY ARM, acknowledging that I am not the peacemaker but that You are. I pray this in recognition that I am in You and You are in me, Lord. Use my body as a tool of deliverance for others.

THURSDAY: I STRETCH FORTH MY ARM, acknowledging that You are all powerful. I don't have the power to bring peace, but You do. Lord God nothing is impossible with You. Make me a vessel of Your peace.

FRIDAY: I STRETCH FORTH MY ARMS as an act of worship and surrender. I yield my will to Your will. I am laying down my agenda and choosing to live for Your agenda.

SATURDAY: I STRETCH FORTH MY ARMS toward heaven, asking that You would teach me how to pray and offer a blessing for others.

Blessed are the Persecuted

THE IMAGE OF GOD: "Remember the word that I said to you, A servant is not greater than his master. If they persecuted Me, they will also persecute you. If they kept My word, they will keep yours also. But all these things they will do to you for My name's sake, because they do not know Him who sent Me" (JN. 15:20-21).

▪ "He came into the very world he created, but the world didn't recognize him. He came to his own people, and even they rejected him. But to all who believed him and accepted him, he gave the right to become children of God" (JN. 1:10-12).

— LOVE YOUR ENEMIES —

THE COMMAND OF CHRIST: "Ye have heard that it hath been said, Thou shalt love thy neighbour, and hate thine enemy. But I say unto you, Love your enemies, bless them that curse you, do good to them that hate you, and pray for them which despitefully use you, and persecute you;" (MATT. 5:43-44 KJV).

▪ "Don't repay evil for evil. Don't retaliate with insults when people insult you. Instead, pay them back with a blessing. That is what God has called you to do, and he will grant you his blessing" (1 PET. 3:8-9).

▪ "Dear friends, never take revenge. Leave that to the righteous anger of God. For the Scriptures say, 'I will take revenge; I will pay them back,' says the LORD. Instead, if your enemies are hungry, feed them. If they are thirsty, give them something to drink. In doing this, you will heap burning coals of shame on their heads. Don't let evil conquer you, but conquer evil by doing good" (ROM. 12:19-21).

- "God blesses you when people mock you and persecute you and lie about you and say all sorts of evil things against you because you are my followers. Be happy about it! Be very glad! For a great reward awaits you in heaven. And remember, the ancient prophets were persecuted in the same way" (MATT. 5:11-12).

- "Who shall not receive a hundredfold now in this time—houses and brothers and sisters and mothers and children and lands, with persecutions—and in the age to come, eternal life" (MK. 10:30).

✓
— LOVE IN THE FACE OF REJECTION —

☐ Have I ever been rejected for my faith in Christ?
☐ What are some less obvious types of persecution?
☐ When persecution comes do I sulk or rejoice?
☐ What can I do to prepare for coming persecution?
☐ Do I pray for God to reveal Himself to my persecutors?
☐ What is a sincere blessing (verbal and or gift) I can give to my enemies?
☐ Have I asked God to make me a channel of His love?
☐ How can I seek peace in the midst of persecution?

FAITH IN ACTION: BE A BLESSING TO YOUR ENEMY

- No need for anger, no place for retaliation, but rather with these eight Beatitudes love your enemies. Your assignment: Do good to your enemies. Be a blessing to the difficult person in your life.

More ideas at GreatWithGod.com

Appeal to Heaven: **Prayer Position for the Persecuted:** leaping for joy.

Sunday: **I Leap For Joy**, believing that You are able to cause all things to work together for good for me because I love You and I am aiming to live according to Your purpose.

Monday: **I Leap For Joy**, understanding that no matter what my enemies plan for evil, You, oh Lord, will turn for good. You are sovereign and I abandon myself to Your providence.

Tuesday: **I Leap For Joy**, realizing that my endurance in trials will be rewarded by You if I do not give up. I rejoice because I know that trials are working a good character in me.

Wednesday: **I Leap For Joy**, acknowledging that I am in You and You are in me. Persecution is evidence of this. Give me an eternal outlook and power to endure tribulation.

Thursday: **I Leap For Joy**, knowing that You are all powerful. You can do anything. So I remind myself that while I can't love my enemies, You can through me.

Friday: **I Leap For Joy** as an act of worship and surrender. I yield my will to Your will. I yield all my rights to success, comfort, and a pain-free life. I want what You want, therefore, I will joyfully endure all persecution that may come my way because I am in You and You are in me. Your will be done and Your kingdom come, not mine.

Saturday: **I Leap For Joy** because Your strength is made perfect in weakness and Your grace is more than enough for me. These victories, these answers of prayer, Lord, these things were made possible because I was in You and You were in me.

AMEN

ABOUT THE COMPOSER

Robert Leatherwood (M.A.) has a passion for mentoring and has spent his lifetime investing in students, men and fathers. He has adopted the commission of Elijah as his own, working to turn the hearts of children to their fathers and the hearts of fathers to their children.

He is the founder of Great with God Ministries which equips mentors worldwide with the tools and resources to make mature disciples of Christ.

He is a missionologist whose vision is to reach all nations in this generation. For the last 17 years he has served as the senior development officer for International Cooperating Ministries (ICM.org).

For hobbies, he is both athlete and artist. In his adult life, he finished the Ironman triathlon competition. As a chalk art evangelist, he enjoys revealing the Secrets to Predicting Destiny.

He does not claim to be the author of this book; this is fundamentally God's word which has simply been uniquely arranged. Many of the praying models are scripture-based and also composed and inspired by the examples of his teachers. The Prayer Wheels are scripture-based and only uniquely illustrated. Composed for the glory of God and that the body of Christ might be inspired and equipped to pursue intimacy with our savior, The Lord Jesus.

Learn more about Great with God Ministries at www. GreatWithGod.com.

Get the *Great With God Ministries* app: *Great with God Pocket Guide.* Visit the website: (**www.GreatWithGod.com**) Equipping disciple makers worldwide with resources to make abiding disciples of Jesus Christ who make abiding disciples of Jesus Christ.

PARTNERING MINISTRIES

International Cooperating Ministries is a partnering ministry; the Mini Bible College is a division of (**ICM.org**), the premier global church development ministry. Get the Mini Bible College App.

Bless Every Home is a partnering ministry. Register with **www.blesseveryhome.com,** a partnering ministry, mobilizing our nation to prayer for every neighbor in every neighborhood in America.

Faith in Action Assignments inspired and adapted by Operation Light Force, a partnering ministry. Visit the website: (**OperationLightForce.com**).

REFERENCES

1   Please note that each of the 52 attributes of God have been synergistically paired with a Command of Christ, and that the Commands of Christ purposefully retain the titles as first introduced to me through the *Commands of Christ Series* as published by the Institute of Basic Life Principles.

2   The Lords Prayer Wheel as an index prayer as taught by Dick Woodward, "The Mini Bible College" audio series, Sermon on the Mount.

3   The Tabernacle Prayer as an index prayer as taught by Dr. Paul Yonggi Cho, "Learn How to Pray," Tabernacle Prayer Message, YouTube.

4   *The God Pocket: He Owns It. You Carry It. Suddenly, Everything Changes* by Bruce Wilkinson and David Kopp. October, 2011. Published by Multnomah Books, Colorado Springs, Colorado 80921.

5   Inspired and adapted from "The Four Spiritual Secrets" as taught by Dick Woodward, interview with Mark Christianson. Also see *The Four Spiritual Secrets* book published by International Cooperating Ministries (**ICM. org**), 2010.

6   Casting Cares Index wheel inspired by Otto Koning, "The Pineapple Series," 2000 audio messages available at Embassy Media.

7   Point of Contact Index inspired from the teaching of Oral Roberts at ORU, "Chapel Service Message," 1984.

8   "Radical Mentoring, Letter From God," www. radicalmentoring.com, dialogue prayer program contained in the commencement retreat.

9   The Ripple Index, The Tabernacle Prayer as an index prayer as taught by Dr. Paul Yonggi Cho, "Learn How to Pray, Tabernacle Prayer Message," YouTube.

10   The Body Position Alignment Index: the source for this index and many of the accompanying daily prayers comes from the "The Body Positions of the Beatitudes" as presented in the "Anger Resolution" seminar published by the Institute in Basic Life Principles as published in the workbook and seminar series (**IBLP.org**). Also available at Embassy Media.